# Praise for *Untangling you: How can I be grateful when I feel so resentful?*

'In this book, Kerry Howells tackles a perplexing issue that humans must face in social life, but which scholars and philosophers have understood poorly – how to disarm complicated feelings of resentment and replace them with gratitude. She deftly empowers readers not just with the skills to reframe difficult feelings of inferiority, of being unappreciated, being excluded or treated unfairly, but also with the skills of inviting gratitude, healing and growth back into their lives so that they can live a truly joyful and optimal life.'

**Giacomo Bono**, Associate Professor and gratitude researcher, California State University, and co-author of *Making Grateful Kids: The Science of Building Character*

'In normal human experience, resentment is the polar opposite of gratitude. Kerry Howells shows us that we are able, paradoxically, to locate and understand in the light of gratitude our own obstinate self-imprisonment in resentment. This is a wise and practical book, the fruit of decades of thoughtful research and experience. There ͏ ͏ not many people who could rightly decide to do ͏ ͏ ͏ '

**Margaret Visser**, author ͏ ͏ ͏ *͏ ͏ ͏ ituals of Gratitude* and *The Ritua* ͏ ͏ ͏

'It was such a pleasure to re͏ ͏ ͏ ͏ ͏ ͏ ͏ ͏ve work which takes gratitude into a differe͏ ͏ ͏ ͏ ͏ or depth and breadth, especially in terms of how it is intertwined with resentment. This has many therapeutic implications. Howells' book is nuanced, uplifting and a much-needed resource in current challenging times.'

**Tayyab Rashid**, PhD, clinical psychologist, University of Toronto Scarborough, and co-author of *Strengths-Based Resilience: A Positive Psychology Program* and *Positive Psychotherapy: Clinician Manual*

'A must-read for anybody who has dealt with conflict in their life, whether personal or professional. The reader will discover the often misunderstood power of gratitude and the role it can play in allowing us to lead a healthy and happier life.'

**Sarah Bolt**, Anti-Discrimination Commissioner, Equal Opportunity Tasmania

'Dr Kerry Howells has written a critically important book for us all. Her book takes the message she so cleverly crafted in her first book, *Gratitude in Education: A Radical View*, and mines ways to recognise how our lives and the lives of all with whom we relate can be enhanced through gratitude. I recommend all to read both this superb book and her first book, and then universally practise gratitude.'

**John Hendry OAM**, Co-founder of Positive Education and UNESCO facilitator on quality relationships

'Resentment can rear its head in so many places in elite sport, and yet there is so little understanding of how to address it effectively and healthily. These concepts, and this book, should form an essential part of coach and athlete development.'

**Laurence Halsted**, Performance Director, Danish Fencing Federation, two-time British Olympic fencer and author of *Becoming a True Athlete: A Practical Philosophy for Flourishing Through Sport*

'The concept of restoring joy of life and reducing friction in relationships is very refreshing. It has provided many positive changes in my personal and family life. It has also helped me improve the culture in my workplace. As a physiotherapist, I was able to recognise resentment as a big challenge in the lives of many of my patients. I believe the concepts of resentment and gratitude explored in this book will bring a new dimension to the treatment of many sufferers of chronic health conditions.'

**Roy Daniell**, MACP, pain and musculoskeletal physiotherapist

'To read this book is a privilege and a gift. It is transformational. Research-based and thought-provoking, it compels us to investigate both our possible current resentments and our ongoing gratitude practice.'

**Bonnie Jeffrey**, School Principal and External School Review Leader

'In an ever-polarising world, Dr Kerry Howells brings clarity to the much-needed social skill of gratitude. Reading this book, I often stopped in thoughtful reflection, especially as I read Kerry's chapter on cross-cultural differences.'

**Michael Grinder**, National Director of NLP in Education and author of *Charisma: The Art of Relationships*

'I found *Untangling you* wonderfully thought-provoking, and the framing of gratitude in the context of resentment really eye-opening and new. It's a brilliant read that I would recommend to athletes, business leaders, teachers and parents.'

**Catherine Bishop**, British Olympic medalist in rowing, diplomat, leadership coach and author of *The Long Win: The Search for a Better Way to Succeed*

'A much-needed book for our times. In my experience as a psycho-therapist, resentment is pervasive yet, paradoxically, so often either underestimated or ignored. Kerry Howells, through her extensive experience and research, has brought it fully into consciousness and richly explores the myriad of ways its toxicity destructively infiltrates our lives.'

**Peter O'Connor**, PhD, psychotherapist and author of *Facing the Fifties: From Denial to Reflection*

'The benefits of deep relational gratitude and developing a gratitude practice, as explored in *Untangling you*, are immeasurable, particularly in deepening relationships and feelings of interconnectedness, and recognising that we can only change ourselves, our attitude and our responses, and that this can have a profound impact on others.'

**Jo Gaha**, Facilitator and Executive Coach, The Potential Project

# Untangling you

## you

### Dr Kerry Howells

First published in 2021 by Major Street Publishing Pty Ltd
E: info@majorstreet.com.au  W: majorstreet.com.au  M: +61 421 707 983

NATIONAL
LIBRARY
OF AUSTRALIA

A catalogue record for this book is available
from the National Library of Australia

Printed book: 978-1-922611-08-6
Ebook: 978-1-922611-09-3

Cover design by Simone Geary
Cover image by Michael Leunig (detail from the cartoon 'How to get through it')
Back cover photo by Perri Wain
Internal design by Production Works
Printed in Australia by Ovato, an Accredited ISO AS/NZS 14001:2004
Environmental Management System Printer.

10 9 8 7 6 5 4 3 2 1

# Contents

| Resentment | Gratitude |
|---|---|
| *Dictionary definition:* | *Dictionary definition:* |
| 'The bitter indignation of being treated unfairly.' | 'The quality of being thankful; readiness to show appreciation for and to return kindness.' |
| *Resentment is explored here more deeply as:* | *Gratitude is explored here more deeply as:* |
| 'A lingering emotion in response to a shock and sense of injustice caused through broken expectations or a sense of being made to feel inferior. More clearly understood in terms of its conceptual opposite: gratitude.' | 'A sincere and meaningful practice in which one acknowledges what one has received and gives back in ways that are not necessarily reciprocal. More clearly understood in terms of its conceptual opposite: resentment.' |
| *Resentment is distinct from:* | *Gratitude is distinct from:* |
| Anger, disappointment, disillusionment and envy | Positivity, optimism, praise and kindness |
| *Resentment thrives in cultures of:* | *Gratitude thrives in cultures of:* |
| Competition, stress, self-centredness, entitlement, isolationism, judgment and perfectionism | Cooperation, calmness, other-centredness, appreciation, interconnectedness, acceptance and humility |

# Introduction

*The deepest principle in human nature
is the craving to be appreciated.*
– William James

I grew up in the 1960s as the eldest of five children, with a father who was often absent and a mother who struggled with her own worries and demons. She always had to work hard to make ends meet, which meant she could bring very little of herself to parenting. I saw the closeness my friends had with their mothers and imagined how it would feel to be nurtured by that intimacy, but all I felt was rejected and neglected because mine had very little energy or time to give to me. My mother and I would argue often. I never felt that she understood me, nor I her. I learned resentment till I knew it well: for me, the taste of resentment was the bitter indignation of being treated unfairly. It coursed through me like a toxic stream until all hope of reconciliation was abandoned. And there we stayed, together but alone, our relationship all but broken, for year after wasted year.

I knew there was a problem – of that I had no doubt – but I had absolutely no idea what to do about it. My pride and stubbornness blocked any way forward. I was not going to be the one to take the initiative to pick up the phone, to make the first move. I was the one who had been wronged; I was the one owed an apology. Until my mother tried to make amends, I was not prepared to forgive her.

I carried this murky feeling with me wherever I went. It cast a dark shadow over all my relationships, and eventually over the parenting of my own daughter. It sat in a pit at the bottom of my stomach. I just couldn't see that there was any way to release myself from it.

Oddly enough, the key to a new understanding of how I felt came from my experience as a young academic teaching a philosophy course to groups of students who had to take my course for their degree. They resented the fact that they had to do a compulsory subject they had no interest in. Eventually, out of sheer frustration, I asked them why they didn't take the opportunity to learn something new. Their response changed my approach to teaching, my career and my life.

They said they wanted to be engaged but they didn't know how. I responded that while they didn't have a choice about doing the course, they did have a choice about how they were going to approach it. So, we started exploring their feelings of resentment and how these were playing out through complaint and dissatisfaction. I invited them to reframe their feelings to ones of gratitude. Surprisingly to me at the time, they wanted to know more.

When I asked what they felt most grateful for, a common answer was 'my parents'. This left me feeling deeply pained that I didn't feel this about my own mother. The ease and enthusiasm with which many of my students spoke about gratitude stood in stark contrast to the glaring absence of gratitude I felt towards my mother. I started to wonder if this was so significant that it blocked my ability to truly feel gratitude for all the other aspects of my life.

This realisation haunted me for some time until I decided to actually do one of the practices I had been recommending to my students: write a gratitude letter. I sat against a tree in a tranquil spot for a good half-hour before I could bring pen to paper. I felt ashamed when I realised that I couldn't remember the last time I had thanked my mother for anything. Where could I start? When I wrote the first line – that I was sorry I hadn't really thanked her for giving me life – the tears started to well up. I started sobbing when I wrote the next line, saying that because she had given me my life, I was now able to be a mother to my own daughter. Then the floodgates opened for many of the other things I was grateful for in my life – my friends, my studies, my students, my love of swimming in the sea – all because of her.

When I visited my mother a week or so after sending her the letter, she hugged me and cried, and thanked me for my words. She told me she felt better than she had for a very long time. I told her that I had the same feeling. As we sat down to dinner, I felt a softening of both our hearts. From that moment, our relationship gradually grew stronger and more harmonious right up until her sudden death six months later.

It was from this point on that I started to truly feel grateful, to feel what I call 'deep gratitude' – not only for my mother, but for many other things in my life. I had tried counselling, meditation and numerous self-development courses to resolve the negative feelings inside me, but I discovered through this experience that it was gratitude that let the light in. It helped us both move past our resentment.

## Why this book?

This initial discovery of the power of gratitude launched me into 25 years of researching its role in education and other fields, and offering workshops and programs to a range of different cohorts: high-school and university students, teachers at all levels of education, including pre-service teachers, elite athletes and their coaches, and healthcare professionals.

For the first decade of exploring the significance of gratitude in education, most of my fellow academics thought I was mad or some kind of weirdo. Fortunately, we've come a long way since then. Hundreds of studies in differing fields have demonstrated the positive benefits of gratitude to our physical, emotional and social wellbeing. Yet there is very little discussion of gratitude in terms of its conceptual opposite: resentment.

Emphasising the benefits of gratitude without also telling the story of when it's a struggle gives a simplistic, one-dimensional view of gratitude. It also leaves us with an impoverished sense of ourselves as human beings. It's only when we experience the discomfort of not being able to find gratitude that a path opens for growth and transformation. We can learn just as much from our 'negative' states as we can from our joys.

One of the most important roles that gratitude can play in our lives is to illuminate where we feel the opposite: it's often the only thing that can bring resentment to light so that we can do something about it and address its negative impact on our lives. If you have underlying resentment about someone, it's impossible to genuinely express gratitude to them.

In the process of trying to sincerely practise gratitude, you become aware of those you feel effortlessly grateful for and those for whom it seems impossible to muster any gratitude – which, for me, was my mother. In the act of writing a gratitude letter to her, I realised how

4

much my resentment had stopped me from seeing any of her goodness or acknowledging what she had done for me as a mother.

Looking at gratitude as the counterpoint to resentment helps to make gratitude more real and attainable. This is why – no matter the context – the questions I most often hear are: 'How can I be grateful when I feel so resentful?' and 'How can I let go of my resentment in order to practise gratitude?'

I have written this book to try to provide some answers to these questions. I know how hard it can be to make the first move when we feel another person has wronged us. However, as I see it, this humble questioning prefaces a commitment to try to change, to try to repair the relationship, to take action rather than waiting around for the other person to change or apologise.

In the following chapters you will see how, as intuitive as these questions are, we can reverse their order: practising gratitude is itself crucial to the freedom of letting go of resentment, and not the other way round. In other words, the question, 'How can I let go of my resentment in order to practise gratitude?' can also be phrased as 'How can I practise gratitude in order to let go of my resentment?'

Although gratitude usually starts with a feeling of delight, appreciation, awe or surprise, deep gratitude is more than a feeling: it is an action. In my case, it wasn't enough to simply *feel* gratitude for my mother, as my resentment towards her was the stronger feeling and had a more powerful pull. It was the action of writing the letter as an expression of gratitude *to* her that caused my gratitude to start to flow. In relationships where we feel resentment, it is when we acknowledge what we are grateful *for*, and then act upon it, that gratitude can have a truly transformative power.

In exploring the interplay between gratitude and resentment, this book focuses on the smaller 'everyday' resentments, not resentment that arises from personal or collective trauma, violence, gross inequities, discrimination, degradation or abuse, or the collective resentment of groups of people who have suffered genocide, historical injustices or wholesale violence for decades. Even though the strategies we explore in this book may be relevant to this kind of resentment, it requires a different kind of context and consideration that is not within the scope of this book.

No doubt you have experienced the everyday kind of resentment in your life: a brother or sister who appeared to be favoured by your parents; a partner who left you for another person; a neighbour who won't deal with their barking dog that keeps you awake for hours; a best friend who betrayed you by sharing your secrets with others; a workmate who was promoted ahead of you (when everyone knew you were the best person for the position); a boss who constantly undermines you; a partner who doesn't do their share of the housework or looking after the children... and the list goes on and on.

These everyday resentments keep simmering away, robbing us of joy and wreaking havoc on our health, relationships and workplaces. Most importantly, they can build over time and contribute to the more traumatic and larger resentments.

They can also dominate many of our decisions. We might not go for that fabulous job because of the resentment we hold towards one of the managers there; or we might not go on that fantastic holiday because of the resentment we feel towards someone who is also going on the trip and who used to be a friend. In my relationship with my mother, my resentment stopped me from going to many family gatherings, particularly as an adult, and I missed out on developing stronger relationships with my siblings and strengthening my feeling of belonging to my family.

This book offers practical strategies to enable you to gracefully start to untangle yourself, bit by bit, and move from resentment towards gratitude. You will:

- discover the important role of gratitude in helping you to identify what resentment looks like and how to attend to its underlying causes
- explore how gratitude can help you take responsibility for the choices you are making in how you respond to situations that would normally give rise to resentment
- uncover the interplay between gratitude and resentment and how this unfolds in the context of daily dilemmas. These include dealing with betrayal, disappointment, bullying, sibling rivalry, perfectionism and workplace conflict
- gain strategies to address self-resentment, as well as the resentment you might experience from others
- acquire more skills and confidence to address some of the difficult relationships in your life
- develop an understanding of how cross-cultural differences influence the dynamic between resentment and gratitude.

I need to emphasise that practising gratitude isn't about trying to replace negative thoughts with positive ones. Gratitude should never be used to try to wipe out our resentment, or as a way of putting a positive veneer over negative situations that are crying out for our attention. My journey with my mother took time. The newfound acknowledgment of the gratitude I had for her gave me the insight and courage to push through my resentment and make my relationship with her more important than my grievances. It wasn't a quick fix, though, as my resentment was quite entrenched and I needed to untangle it over time.

As the book title suggests, think of addressing your resentments as if they were a tangled ball of string. Some parts are harder to untangle because one instance of deep-seated resentment is often intertwined with resentment in other relationships. Other parts may just need a slight pull and the ball will start to untangle quite easily.

If you're wondering where to begin, I strongly suggest you start with some of these easier situations and build up your skills, so that later you can work on the tangles that are harder to loosen. If you are filled with pain or anxiety from even contemplating a difficult relationship, it's clear that for now it should be left alone. You may also feel the need to seek professional support.

The following chapters are aimed to help you to shift the dynamics of relationships that have been stuck in pain for a long time, even decades. I encourage you to read each chapter in order, as each builds upon the understanding and strategies of the previous chapters.

My sincere hope is that as you practise gratitude through the strategies you learn in this book, you discover the significant benefit this has on your relationships with others and yourself. In fact, I feel that gratitude is one of the most powerful ways of helping us to achieve sustainable health, harmony and peaceful coexistence.

# Chapter 1

## Why gratitude?

*He who has a why can endure any how...*
– Friedrich Nietzsche

I'm often asked in gratitude workshops why we would even bother to think about being grateful to our 'enemies'. Why should we try to be friends with everyone, or to love every one of our workmates? Life just doesn't work like that. Besides, that's just being phony, right? Surely it makes more sense just to keep in our inner circle those we naturally gravitate to and feel comfortable with, and stay away from those we resent?

I'm not arguing here that all relationships in our lives should have the same level of closeness or that we should attempt the impossible task of loving all people equally. What I am saying is that, whether we like it or not, we are always in relationship with others, and relationships in our lives really matter. We intuitively know this because of how much we suffer when they are not working – as I discovered with my mother. No matter how much we try to protect ourselves by pushing people away, if we are in a relationship that is unresolved or carries a lot of resentment, then deep in our subconscious it is very likely to be eating away at us.

This was the case for Sarah, who had recently moved into a flat to share with her friend Dave. Sarah and Dave had become very good mates at school and were part of a large friendship group who went everywhere together – camping, clubbing, eating out, and so on. The differences between them in terms of values and habits only surfaced when they moved into the flat. Sarah – quite a neat, sensitive and careful person – was the opposite to Dave. An art student, he was protective of his 'free spirit' and need for lots of flexibility to express his creativity. In the past this had been something Sarah loved about him, but living with it was quite a different story. Dave would rebel against any routine as he tried to avoid committing to doing anything at a particular time. To keep Sarah happy, he said yes to the roster Sarah tried to introduce to keep the house clean and in order, but was half-hearted both in his agreement and in doing the tasks.

Things were coming to a head when Sarah struggled with the rubbish bins three weeks in a row, a task Dave had next to his name on their supposedly agreed-upon roster. When she was at the shops buying toilet paper for the fifth time in as many weeks, she was furious. She found herself getting upset in the shower one morning because of the mould in the corner that Dave had promised he would get rid of weeks ago. This was exacerbated by the fact that he had been late with his share of the rent twice. Sarah felt used and disrespected. What frustrated her most was that Dave seemed to be oblivious to the pain he was causing her. Over time, Sarah felt herself becoming cold, indifferent and withdrawn. She was also very sad that, for her, their friendship had soured.

Dave was completely oblivious to all this. A big-picture person who didn't notice or care much about details, he just didn't think these things were such a big deal. For him, what was important was that they were sharing a flat, eating together and having conversations about what had happened that day. Dave thought that Sarah's stress was just because she was studying hard for her university exams.

Sarah, on the other hand, was having trouble sleeping, going over all the details of what Dave didn't do that he had said he would do, and fretting about how to bring it up with him so that it didn't damage the relationship or cause him to think less of her. She was paranoid that if she upset Dave, the news of their conflict would spread to their friendship group. As they all adored Dave, she feared they would take his side and see her as too pedantic, a clean freak, or controlling.

Eventually Sarah tried to bring up her grievances with Dave, but she was too nervous and tongue-tied to do so successfully. She was anxious that her carefully prepared speech would go wrong. After a few more weeks of barely tolerating the situation, she decided it was time to move out so that she could regain her peace of mind and get on with her studies.

Was there another way through the conflict that didn't involve Sarah having to give up her flat, and her friendship with Dave and possibly with their wider group?

## Finding your 'why'

Sarah's father had started to implement gratitude as a practice with his work team after attending one of my workshops, a few months before Sarah came to him in tears about her dilemma. As he started to rave about how much his gratitude had helped him feel more positive in his workplace, enthusiastically telling Sarah how it might help her situation with Dave, Sarah looked at him with horror. Gratitude? Are you kidding? Hadn't he heard a word she had said about how disrespected and furious she felt? How could he possibly think that she could just put all this aside and be grateful to Dave?

Sarah was absolutely right. As mentioned, it never works to try to replace resentment with gratitude. What she needed in that moment was for her pain to be acknowledged. She also needed a strong reason to even contemplate gratitude as a way forward. Any comment from a third party in that moment needed to speak to Sarah's world, to make sense in the context of what *she* was dealing with. It wasn't enough that gratitude had worked in another's world – in this case, her father's.

It's certainly easier to see the relevance of gratitude in situations where it's natural or relatively easy to be spontaneously thankful. Gratitude helps you feel enlivened when you are taking in a beautiful sunrise. It helps you to have a more restful sleep if you write down what you are grateful for at the end of your day. A lot of contemporary research is showing us that gratitude enhances our physical and emotional wellbeing. However, finding the sense in looking for gratitude when you feel another person has hurt you can be very tough. Society wouldn't blame you for not even trying, or for walking away and banishing that relationship completely from your life – as Sarah was about to do.

Finding reasons to even bother to do things differently is a crucial first step in the move from resentment towards gratitude. Your personal 'why' may well be quite different from another person's. It will be influenced by your values, faith, gender, race or personality.

What is crucial is that you find reasons that strongly resonate with you. That's the beauty of gratitude. We all come to it from different angles and for different reasons.

One of the many pluses for dealing with the resentment I had towards my mother was that I then felt I would have some integrity with my students when inviting them to practise gratitude. When I looked more deeply, I found my 'why' was related to a wider sense of integrity in regard to how gratitude in difficult relationships contributes to a better world. This reason for why gratitude is important still drives me today, and indeed is the main reason for writing this book. It's also why I am motivated to keep working on moving from resentment towards gratitude in my own life.

## Gratitude helps us feel more connected to others

A big motivation for Sarah to work on her conflict with Dave was that she didn't want to lose her connection with him and her wider friendship group. Gratitude by its very nature invites us to take a bigger perspective where we are not only thinking about ourselves but about our connectedness with others. Gratitude has a strong awakening power that helps us to realise our interdependence, and to see the value of another person and what we've received from them. We connect with another – or others – who made this moment, who were part of bringing this opportunity into being. When we thank someone, we are really saying, 'I humbly recognise that without your gift, I would not have this... I would not be this...' Gratitude gathers together and entwines giver, receiver and gift.[1]

In fact, numerous research studies have demonstrated the powerful role gratitude has in building and maintaining relationships.[2, 3, 4, 5, 6]

This is aptly caught in sociologist Georg Simmel's stance that gratitude is the most important cohesive element for society. He calls it 'the moral memory of mankind,' the bridge connecting one human being with another, and says, 'If every grateful action, which lingers on from good turns received in the past, were suddenly eliminated, society (at least as we know it) would break apart.'[7]

We experience a certain unrest, perhaps at a deep subconscious level, when we neglect to express our gratitude to someone who has given us something. In the case of my mother, while my resentment towards her ate up my gratitude for many years, there was still a gnawing feeling that I should be grateful to her, even though I couldn't because I felt so hurt.

When you think about it, there's always something we can find that another has given us. It can be impersonal, like the person who sold us the nice bananas we are eating, or those who grew them or transported them to the shops. Then, at the other end of the spectrum, there is the gratitude we feel towards the people we are closest to.

The etymology of the word 'relationship' shows us that historically it meant 'connection, correspondence' as well as 'act of telling', from Anglo-French: *relacioun*; and from Latin: *relationem* – 'a bringing back, restoring, a report, a proposition'. Gratitude has an amazing power to help us to connect with others. The words 'thank you', when uttered sincerely, contain a particular kind of 'correspondence'. When we receive thanks from another, we are often motivated to return this gratitude to that person or give it to someone else. In healthy relationships, this giving-and-receiving cycle is circulating much of the time. When we recognise another through genuine or deep gratitude – without wanting anything in return – we are touching a part of the connection that cannot be touched in any other way. We acknowledge the worth and value of that person, and they are able to see more of this in themselves. We help them flourish and we help the relationship flourish.

## Gratitude helps us remember the good

Sarah's sense of reconnection with Dave was forged during her next conversation with her father. Fortunately, Sarah's father started to understand how difficult it was for her to see the relevance of gratitude in this situation with Dave. Sarah's expectations of how wonderful it would be to be flatmates with Dave had not been met, and she now found it very hard to see anything good in him. After listening attentively, Sarah's father expressed his disappointment that the friendship had deteriorated to such an extent. He talked about all the great times that she and Dave had had together – the school camping trips, the parties – and all of the good qualities he could see in Dave. As Sarah listened, she recognised that the hardships of the past six months had made her forget. The memory of the good times had been eaten up by her resentment. Her father's words didn't take away from her very real frustration about the unfair division of tasks in their household, but they helped her find a broader context for it.

When we look at the scientific research, it's perfectly understandable why this happened for Sarah and would likely happen for most of us. In his 'amplification theory of gratitude', renowned gratitude researcher Phillip Watkins cites the work of Roy Baumeister and his colleagues who showed that, evolutionarily speaking, no matter how much we want to focus on the good, 'bad is stronger than good'.[8] This doesn't mean that bad people are stronger than good people, but rather that 'generally speaking, bad events, bad comments, bad interactions, bad thoughts, and bad memories have a more powerful psychological impact on us than do good events.'[9]

However, the amplification theory shows that more than any other emotion, gratitude has the power to make the good stronger than the bad. When we are grateful, Watkins argues, we amplify our awareness of beneficial and positive events, of the memories of these events, and of the good in others.[10] It follows, then, that the more we practise gratitude, the weaker the hold of the bad thoughts and memories will be, and the greater our capacity to see a bigger picture that includes both the bad and the good.

Again, amplifying the good by calling to mind things to be grateful for isn't about replacing bad thoughts or feelings with good ones. As you will read in the following chapters, in the case of strong resentment – and particularly that which is harboured for a long time – there are steps that need to be taken before we can even begin to be grateful. In helping us to remember what we have received in the past, gratitude can often be the starting point in helping us to forgive. It takes courage and humility, but gratitude helps to orientate us towards the good in the other person, and therefore to see beyond what we consider to be the bad.

Gratitude also provides a strong protective power, so that it's less likely for the bad to take hold, or for negative feelings arising in a particular moment to morph into long-term resentment. If Sarah had been consciously practising gratitude towards Dave, she most probably would have been able to perceive Dave's actions differently. Sarah might have focused more on all the meals he had cooked, the takeaways he had bought, the lively conversations after a dull day of studying. All of this had been nullified by her resentment and only being able to see what Dave *hadn't* done.

Through her father's reminder of all Dave's good points, Sarah was able to amplify the good she saw in Dave. This gradually gave her a new perspective; she wasn't so consumed by her resentment and now had some hope for a way forward. By focusing more on what she was grateful for in her relationship with Dave, she was able to remember how their friendship had enriched her; how he had stood up for her when others were giving her a hard time; how he had actually contributed to looking after the flat in his own way.

## Gratitude helps us to feel calm

Part of Sarah's dilemma with Dave had been that her resentment made her feel like an unreasonable, controlling and overly emotional person, and it stopped her from communicating calmly and rationally. This really unsettled her, and she couldn't focus on her studies. However, when she found her way back to a sense of gratitude for Dave, she felt calmer.

In my research, which has involved numerous case studies in a range of different contexts, a prominent and recurring theme is that people feel calmer when they consciously practise gratitude.[11, 12] According to the participants' own responses, gratitude has helped them gain a clearer perspective, grown their sense of interconnectedness, and helped them solve a conflict they felt stuck in. So, another 'why' for gratitude is that it can help us stay calm.

What is it about gratitude that brings us into a calmer state? How can becoming more open to what we receive from others and the world around us, and expressing this gratitude in action, give us the tranquillity that most of us are seeking?

As we will explore in the following section, gratitude helps us feel well, and when we are well, we are able to lead a more grateful life. We have more internal peace.

Gratitude gives us a sense of abundance. We turn our attention to what we already have rather than striving for more, or comparing ourselves with others, or wishing things were otherwise. We feel that we have more than enough. We are more than enough.

Gratitude brings us more fully into the present moment and frees us from worry about the past or from fretting about the future. In a way that's self-reinforcing, the joy that the present moment gives us when we are in a state of gratitude has a generative power.

Moreover, there is a certain unrest we feel at a deep, subconscious level if we don't express gratitude to those to whom we know we should be grateful. We might be too busy or distracted and not immediately act on what we know, at the core of our being, we should be doing – the thanks that should be said or expressed. Then time passes and we may feel it's too late. This can cause ongoing discontent.

Gratitude can also help us feel calmer because, by practising it consciously, we are taking greater control of our response to situations that arise, including in times of adversity. We are claiming more of a choice in how we act and show up in the world. We realise that we can't change others and come to see that this is not our responsibility. However, we can change ourselves. As you will discover in the following chapters, when we move from resentment towards gratitude, we can feel calmer, because we feel more ownership over the choices we are making and can have a renewed focus on what is achievable.

## Gratitude helps us to stay well

We also saw in Sarah's case that her resentment was causing her to feel stressed and to have trouble sleeping. Another motivation to practise gratitude in difficult relationships is that when we are grateful, we feel better mentally, emotionally and physically. The exact opposite is the case when we feel resentful. We can learn a lot about our health by seeing how these two states manifest in our lives.

A poignant experience of this for me has been in my collaboration with an oncology professor to investigate the relevance of gratitude in enhancing the quality of end-of-life care for cancer patients. This professor initiated our research project because he'd noticed the difference an attitude of gratitude had made to his patients in contrast to an attitude of resentment.

Generally speaking, many patients – young and old – are resentful about how their dignity and sense of worth in the world is suddenly crushed by the indignity of an incurable disease. They're resentful about needing to depend on others. They're resentful about the pity they often unwittingly receive from those who care for them. They're resentful that they're dying, or at risk of dying, when those around them are well. They're resentful about medical bureaucracy and the countless forms they need to fill in. Then there's also self-resentment. Most patients don't like the resentment that their illness brings to the surface, but they feel powerless to do anything about it.

This professor observed that with his cancer patients, their resentment seemed to be a significant factor in the way they responded to treatment. In contrast, patients with the same disease, and of the same age and background, seemed better able to manage their extensive treatments when they had a grateful attitude. A number of clinical studies in other medical fields corroborate this observation.[13, 14, 15]

Clearly, the oncology professor is not saying that gratitude has the capacity to cure cancer, but he feels strongly that it's an important factor in giving cancer patients the best possible quality of life, whatever course the disease takes.

Recent developments in consciousness research and cognitive neuroscience have led to numerous clinical studies demonstrating that gratitude greatly enhances our wellbeing. For example, with regard to psychological health, several studies have shown that having a grateful disposition offers some protection against depression and anxiety as well as stress and trauma.[16, 17, 18, 19, 20, 21] Research has also indicated that gratitude can lead to more refreshing sleep, improved heart health and immune system functioning, and reduces a range of other physical symptoms; it also improves mood and lowers fatigue, and may protect against burnout.[22] A recent study suggests that expressing gratitude can motivate people to put more effort into a range of positive behaviours such as exercising, building relationships, helping others and other proactive behaviours that lead to self-improvement.[23]

Gratitude also helps us to be more resilient. We need resilience in order to withstand the effects of our resentment, and to build fortitude so that it can take less of a hold. Research shows that gratitude promotes positive reappraisal and healthy coping.[24, 25] It also broadens and builds social and cognitive resources.[26]

Although research on the health implications of resentment is still in its infancy, and not nearly as prolific as that on gratitude, some evidence shows that resentment has the opposite effect on our wellbeing. As the philosopher Friedrich Nietzsche wrote:

'Nothing burns one up faster than the effects of resentment. [...] No reaction could be more disadvantageous for the exhausted;

such effects involve a rapid consumption of nervous energy, a pathological increase of harmful excretions – for example the gall bladder into the stomach.'[27]

In one of the few books covering resentment research – *On resentment: Past and present* – various contributors describe the negative effects of resentment as including anxiety, depression and embitterment. One of the authors, Pilar León-Sanz, historian of medicine and medical ethics, summarises the psychosomatic impacts of resentment as detailed in more than 270 articles that were published in the field of psychosomatic medicine during the period from 1939 to 1960. She concluded that these studies showed that resentment could be implicated in the development of ulcers, gastric disorders, heartburn, cardio-respiratory symptoms, cardiac disease, intolerance to exercise, headache, backache, joint pain, insomnia and stress.[28]

Research on unforgiveness and rumination shows a close correlation with resentment.[29] For example, neuroscientist Emiliano Ricciardi and his colleagues have provided a summary of the impact of the erosion of health that arises from these factors. This includes impoverished sleep, alteration of cardiovascular activity, stimulation of stress-related hormones and, over time, the development of clinical conditions including depression.[30] In other studies, maintaining unforgiveness is associated with stress that accelerates the ageing process and leads to a variety of diseases.[31] Likewise, rumination (medically defined as obsessive thinking about an idea, situation or choice[32]) has been found to have a negative impact on healthy coping and to be a contributing factor in chronic illnesses such as heart disease and cancer.[33]

Indeed, it's common to find the physical impact of resentment expressed in our everyday language, such as when we complain about someone being a 'pain in the neck', or that we feel hurt by another 'in the pit of our stomach', or that someone makes our head hurt, or has 'hardened our heart' or left us feeling 'broken-hearted'.

## Our 'why' should never be to change another

Coming back to the situation with Sarah and Dave, Sarah's newfound gratitude for Dave led her to the decision not to move out. In the weeks that followed, she noticed that she felt less stressed, was sleeping better and could concentrate more on her studies.

But you might well be asking here whether Dave changed his behaviour or not. It's true that he would most likely have needed to make some changes for the household dynamic to evolve to a more equitable sharing of tasks. Some of the stories you will read in other chapters have resolutions whereby when one person practises gratitude, there is an immediate grateful response from the other person – as was the case with my mother. This is wonderful when it happens, but it is not always the outcome. My choice in covering only one side of the story in relation to Sarah is very deliberate. My firm belief is that gratitude is necessarily non-reciprocal. Even with my mother, if I had wanted something from her when writing a letter of gratitude – wanting her to become more loving towards me or for her to change in some way, for instance – my gratitude would have been conditional and therefore much less powerful. I was very moved by my mother's response to the letter and the harmony that ensued. This amplified my feeling of gratitude. However, such outcomes were accompanied by feelings of surprise: I certainly wasn't expecting them.

In other words, we don't practise gratitude so that someone else will respond in a certain way, or so that we can change them or make them feel grateful towards us. This should never be our reason. If we use another person's gratitude as a yardstick for the success or impact of our own gratitude, we are more often than not going to be disappointed, and this can become a seed of further resentment because they aren't acting as we hoped they would.

Besides, our actions of gratitude may also live on in ways that we may never know, or which we only find out about much later. In her book *Teaching Outside the Box*, LouAnne Johnson captures this in her story of a person who ran a private detective agency and was asked about the most common reason people hire private detectives. We might think that it would be to investigate people who are having affairs, but no. After interviewing over 150 detectives in his agency, the most common request was for help to find a former teacher so that they could thank them![34]

For Sarah to develop her gratitude, she needed to move past how it might affect Dave or change his behaviour. Instead, her focus for why she was practising needed to be to change *herself*: to keep her friendship, to help her to become kinder and have greater integrity, to amplify the good she perceived in Dave and her own life, and to become more skilled in relationships and dealing with situations of conflict.

However, although Sarah had discovered her reasons for why she needed to start untangling the difficulties she was experiencing with Dave, this didn't mean that all of the differences and the conflict between her and Dave just completely disappeared. Indeed, even though there'd been some untangling, and Sarah's gratitude for Dave was partially restored, her newfound gratitude was performing one of its most important roles: to illuminate where it is absent. If they were to keep on sharing their flat – and indeed, from Sarah's perspective, if their friendship were to be more robust and honest – there were many things that needed to be said, discussed and hopefully agreed on.

The situation we have been exploring in this chapter is fairly straightforward, and it may be easy to envisage how gratitude can be revived enough to be able to let go of resentment. What is less straightforward are the things that undermine this – those murky, uncomfortable and often hidden feelings that make gratitude seem totally inaccessible, despite knowing that it's important.

As the following chapter explores, the first step in finding our way forward in these instances is to recognise resentment. By identifying the underlying characteristics of resentment, we are able to have a clearer sense of what it looks, feels and sounds like, and therefore to be in a position to do something about it.

# Characteristics of deep gratitude

❖ Builds and maintains relationships

❖ Starts with a feeling of delight, appreciation, awe or surprise

❖ Deepens when expressed through action

❖ Needs to be acted on and practised, not just thought about
  or felt

❖ Generates more gratitude

❖ Grows deeper over time

❖ Cultivates a sense of interconnectedness and interdependence

❖ Involves a dynamic of giving *and* receiving

❖ Does not expect anything in return or any change in another

❖ Amplifies our awareness of the good in others

❖ Helps us to see where we have resentment

❖ Influences us and the world in ways we may never realise

# Chapter 2

## Identifying our resentment

*Resentment is like drinking poison and then*
*hoping it will kill your enemies.*

– Nelson Mandela

## Resentment hides

Gratitude has an amazing power to illuminate where it is missing, and in particular where its opposite – resentment – is residing. We can start to notice this in situations where we want to express gratitude but find it hard to do so authentically because we are actually feeling pain or a reticence of some kind. I often describe this as 'murky', because we know something isn't quite right, but it's often hard to give it a name or to acknowledge it fully to ourselves, let alone the other person.

In fact, it's often difficult to recognise that we even have resentment, because by nature it's hidden. As philosopher Juan Bernal says, 'The standard for resentment, in interpersonal relationships, should not be talked about; resentment should be kept secret, even from oneself.'[1] We might be too afraid to admit that we are resentful because we want to keep our image of being a nice and positive person, or we don't want to upset the status quo.

Even though they also aren't pleasant, other negative emotions such as jealousy, anger, frustration and disappointment are much more 'upfront', more conscious, than feelings of resentment. They are often easier to talk about with others because our reactions seem perfectly reasonable and have more social acceptance. Feeling outraged at being treated badly as a casual employee seems completely justifiable. Being angry and frustrated over political inaction in the face of climate change is considered an acceptable stance. Voicing disgust and outrage about the damage done by domestic violence is a genuine response, validated by community views.

Resentment, though, often carries a sense of shame. It exposes us; it makes us seem a bit weak, or not the sort of person we would like to think we are or would like others to see us as. Why haven't we moved on? Why are we holding on to such a seemingly small thing for such a long time? Sometimes it can seem quite irrational that it can hurt us so deeply. The shame and guilt add a layer of complexity to our capacity to identify resentment.

We might also be ashamed about feeling resentment towards those to whom we think we should be grateful. We can be stuck in what I call the 'sticky web of gratitude', where we are torn between a sense of what we might owe someone for the good we have received from them and the resentment we experience because they have hurt us. Resentment is usually the stronger feeling here, but we tend to hide it because we think we should be grateful. This sticky web is very prevalent in romantic relationships. We might live with the constant reminders of what our partner has done for us in the past and all we are grateful for in them. However, this can prevent us from being honest with ourselves about needing to address areas where we feel they have let us down or caused us pain.

Another aspect of the sticky web of gratitude is our pervading sense that, no matter how much gratitude we may feel towards the other person, if we feel they have caused our resentment, it's them who should be doing the work, not us. We might settle for a mediocre or insincere level of gratitude to them – which, by the way, isn't really gratitude – and be waiting around for them to recognise our pain and do something about it. This waiting game can go on for months or even years. In the meantime, we have hidden our resentment by normalising it or deciding to settle for less in the relationship – all in the name of 'gratitude'.

Often there's a fear that if we revisit old pain or bitterness, we're just digging up old wounds. Furthermore, if we think about the consequences of talking to the other person about it, we'd likely be afraid of what they might do – particularly if they are in a position of power. To confront someone who has hurt us can be very frightening. We might not trust ourselves to deal with the situation rationally and calmly, so maybe it's better, we say to ourselves, just to leave it as it is. If we do this over time, we keep normalising it until we can't recognise that we are resentful. Our resentment might also be so longstanding that it has become part of our way of being, our personality. We may not even see it as something we have a choice over.

Sure, some resentments are not hidden, like those associated with injustices inflicted by traumatic events. It's much easier to voice this kind of resentment, as it is usually considered to be righteous and totally reasonable. In these cases, resentment is likely thought of – often with public agreement – as the most appropriate response, and it carries no shame. Public outcries of resentment about racial prejudice or religious intolerance are cases in point.

However, these larger resentments can drown out or minimise the significance of smaller, everyday resentments. Part of our shame in holding on to smaller resentments is that they seem insignificant compared to the larger injustices of the world. Again, most of what's been written about resentment discusses it in light of larger, more traumatic resentments, and the smaller ones receive much less attention.

In order for resentment to come out of hiding, we need to acknowledge it. We need to find ways of giving our resentment a voice, a shape, a place at the table for discussion, without shame or guilt, without self-judgment or the judgment of others. Only then can we see how much our resentment is robbing us of our gratitude and destroying our relationships. In this chapter, we look at some of the main characteristics of resentment so that we are better able to identify our own resentments. One of the first places to look for our resentment is where we find it impossible to feel grateful.

## Resentment negates gratitude

A classic example of resentment can be found in a story I heard about the relationship between Jeremy and his mother Gwen. Gwen had lived in a nursing home for the past decade. Jeremy dreaded going to visit his mother (and then felt guilty that he felt that way). Their conversations would usually come around to Gwen harping on about how her husband – Jeremy's father – had so heartlessly ended their marriage to run off with '*that* woman' who was much younger than Gwen. She went on and on with the same old stories about the beautiful home they'd had to sell, the school Jeremy had had to switch to, the friends she'd lost, and how their lives could have been so much better if her husband had 'done the right thing'.

Gwen's ongoing sense of betrayal and hurt was enormous and, to a degree, understandable. But it had dominated her life for the past 30 years. Not just 5 years, not 10, not 20, but 30 years! Gwen couldn't let go of the pain of that betrayal. Her feelings couldn't be 're-sent' because the pain was stuck. Resentment had seeped into her very bones. It had poisoned her mind – and poisoned the people close to her as well.

When her husband told her that he was leaving the marriage, Gwen was jealous, angry, disappointed, frustrated, sad and in total shock. She'd had no idea that he would hurt her so much. These painful thoughts lingered, and went round and round in her head, night after night, year after year, and eventually her feelings turned into a profound pattern of resentment.

Gwen viewed other events in her life through this lens of resentment, and it didn't take much for her to feel disappointed if things didn't go her way. Eventually her bitterness became a defining part of her life and her identity. As philosopher Friedrich Nietzsche said, 'Nothing on earth consumes a man more quickly than the passion of resentment.' Gwen was so consumed by resentment that she developed the fixed persona of 'a resentful person'.

Gwen's bitterness usually escalated around Christmas time, because her husband had chosen Christmas Eve to announce that he was leaving. Her litany of complaints to Jeremy was predictable: 'Not another Christmas I have to get through... Here we go again, another sad and miserable Christmas, thanks to your father,' and so on. Most of the time, Gwen was so consumed by her anger that she couldn't see or feel anyone else's pain. Jeremy's children and wife found it unbearable. Every year, they begged for a 'Gwen-free Christmas'. They were all sick of the way Gwen's resentment raised its head and polluted the whole holiday, every single year.

Not only did Gwen's family find her hard going, so did most of the carers in her nursing home. She was known for her bitter and snide remarks if any of them were even slightly late in attending to her needs or didn't do something according to her standards. In all the years she was there, Gwen hardly ever offered any appreciation for anything anyone did for her. This, in turn, made the staff less likely to want to spend time with her.

Jeremy had tried to remind his mother that his father wasn't all bad. There had been some good years, and he did have some good qualities. He felt most saddened by the fact that Gwen couldn't recognise that one of the good things that had happened was Jeremy himself. But Gwen's resentment was so huge it obliterated any possibility of feeling gratitude for anything that had happened before her husband left the marriage.

For her own sake, and that of himself and his family, Jeremy would beg his mother to forgive his father, to let go of all this pain and blame. But Gwen would get hurt or angry at the mere suggestion. She accused Jeremy of being insensitive and belittling her pain. And so, the resentment continued to grow.

## Resentment ruminates

Philosopher Amélie Rorty describes resentment thus: '...it feeds itself on the past, chewing over painful memories of humiliations, insults and injuries, regurgitating them until their very bitterness acquires a savoury taste'.[2]

Have you ever felt so hurt by someone that you think you'll never be able to let the pain go? As with Gwen, it can stick with you for years. It haunts you at night when there is nothing to distract you. Your mind keeps going over and over what happened. You ruminate, trying to process the pain, the shock, hoping to make sense of it – but you can't. During the day you go over everything again with anyone who'll listen, trying to make sense of being so let down. You seek the validation of others to reassure yourself that it is not just you who is disgusted, angry or surprised about this situation.

The word 'resentment' comes from the Old French word *resentir*, which means 'the re-experiencing of a strong feeling'.[3] Two distinguishing features of resentment are that it causes us to ruminate – that is, to go over and over the situation in our minds – and that it lingers over time.

When Gwen's husband walked out of their marriage, she didn't hold back. She expressed her shock, hurt and anger to anyone who would listen. But because she wasn't able to express these feelings directly to her husband – the source of her pain – she couldn't let go of her sense of injustice at his actions, and her feelings became lodged as resentment. What's more, she felt powerless to do anything to change the situation. Gwen's emotions were not able to be *e-motions* – energy in motion – because she was stuck in this pain.

It's not a single emotion that makes up resentment but a mixture. Warren TenHouten, a sociology professor, calls this the 'tertiary-level' nature of resentment, meaning that it's a combination of anger, disgust and surprise.[4] The kind of surprise we are talking about here is not pleasant. It's the kind of shock that Gwen experienced: deep shock that a person could behave in such a way, or that all is not as it seems. And it's this shock that keeps our resentment so trapped.

Because resentment is stuck emotion and we are not able to move on from the pain, it becomes a magnet for other resentments as it grows and festers. You might have experienced this yourself: lying awake at night going over and over a current resentment, finding that other resentments seem to find their way into your mind. If you don't do anything about the resentment, it might cause insomnia and a range of other physical and mental illnesses as described in Chapter 1.

As we can see from Gwen's case, her rumination became habitual and then her resentment became her whole personality, the whole principle by which she lived her life and related to others – even those who had nothing to do with her pain. When resentment becomes our way of being in the world, the rumination not only resides in our emotions or thoughts, but we can develop a whole pathology of resentment.

## Resentment seeks justice

So, what if Gwen forgave her husband? Would this be enough for her to get rid of her resentment? It's unlikely, because another characteristic of resentment is that we say we have forgiven the person but a lingering feeling of ill will prevails.[5] In other words, unless we can find a way to both forgive and forget, we are bound to the memory of the perceived wrongdoing and we can't move on.

If we are guided, for instance, by John F. Kennedy's suggestion to 'Forgive your enemies, but never forget their names,' this allows our resentment to sit side by side with our forgiveness. However, such a stance undermines the power of forgiveness, and in some cases its authenticity. Our 'not forgetting' can translate into a decision to hold on to the painful emotions.

We then have to question the true sincerity and power of such forgiveness when it is offered to us. You've probably experienced situations where a person says they forgive you, but it comes with a pained expression, or an inability to look at you, or a knowledge that this person continues to backbite or defame you. As a result, you don't really feel forgiven.

One of the main reasons why we say we will forgive but never forget is that at the core of resentment is our need to seek justice. It's our way of righting the wrong. We believe that in responding with resentment, we are taking a moral stance about the injustice we feel has occurred. In fact, some have even called resentment 'an emotion of justice'.[6]

For Gwen, she felt that giving up her resentment would amount to letting her ex-husband off the hook – that she accepted his unjust and injurious actions or was condoning his betrayal of her. Gwen's resentment was a way of proclaiming to herself and others that she knew right from wrong, and that she was clearly right and her ex-husband was clearly wrong.

However, it's an illusion that resentment will somehow bring justice to the situation and hurt the other person. In reality, it brings nothing but harm to ourselves and all those affected by our resentment. This is why Nelson Mandela's statement is so apt: 'resentment is like drinking poison and then hoping it will kill your enemies.' Even though Gwen felt that her strong emotions of resentment were entirely justified, in fact her husband had moved on. He was living a new life and, after 30 years, quite possibly not feeling much guilt about the pain he had caused her.

Again, because resentment seeks justice, forgiving is unlikely to be enough to be able to let go of the pain. The sense of injustice is the thing that makes it hard for us to truly forgive. In its pursuit of justice, resentment keeps us bound to the memory of the perceived wrongdoing and we can't move on.

There's another angle to this as well. When we are consumed by resentment and endlessly ruminate on a perceived injustice, it's almost impossible to give the person whom we feel has wronged us a fair go. Our shock and bitter disappointment often blocks our capacity to see things from the other person's perspective. Resentment tends to make us quick to protect ourselves and, often in the name of justice, put up all kinds of barriers to being able to perceive things otherwise. It can make us hypersensitive and perhaps unable to see a way forward. We might therefore tell ourselves that it's easier just to leave the tangled relationship alone and keep suppressing – and hiding – our resentment.

## Resentment leads to powerlessness

We saw Jeremy plead with Gwen to choose otherwise – to forgive, to appreciate happier times before 'the event' when her husband left her. He lived in eternal hope that one day she would realise she had a choice in how to respond. It was, in fact, her entrenched perceived inability to choose otherwise that irked Jeremy the most.

When we have long-term resentment, it controls the way we see the world, and we gather evidence that reinforces the story that causes the pain that we feel. Because resentment is deeply lodged, it fixes our world view in place. The wrongdoing of another becomes our whole story, and there is no room for anything else. As was the case for Gwen, to suggest that we choose otherwise can feel like an assault on our whole identity.

A characteristic of resentment is that we feel powerless to choose another state. In actual fact, much of the time, we blame the other person not only for the perceived wrongdoing but also for making us feel stuck in resentment. We are in a cycle of toxic *reaction* rather than being able to take action to choose otherwise. Consequently, resentment carries with it this sense of having no other choice, characterised by blame and feeling as if we are a total victim of the other person's wrongdoing. To take responsibility for our state – and our reactions – can feel like we are letting the other person off the hook or forgiving them in some way, and again threaten our sense of the injustice of the situation.

Acknowledging that you feel resentment *and* that you have the power to choose otherwise are the most important things you can do to take action. This was the course that Jeremy chose. Eventually he had to accept that it was almost certainly a lost cause to expect his 81-year-old mother to change. What Jeremy could do was learn from this experience so his own resentment towards his mother didn't fester, and so that he didn't respond to disappointments in his own life in such a powerless and destructive way.

## Resentment festers

If you have resentment, has hiding it ever helped it go away? Suppressing resentment just makes the situation worse. We can't just wait around hoping that it will go away by itself or over time, because by nature, it doesn't. It festers. Resentment gathers energy around it. In wanting to gather others around us who reinforce our sense of the injustices, we are likely to attract others who are also harbouring their own resentments.

As mentioned, because Gwen's original shock about the betrayal lodged itself so deeply within her and eventually influenced her whole way of being in the world, she saw many other things in her life through this lens. She was on the lookout for other instances of disappointment or betrayal and made these big in her own mind, confirming her view that the world was unjust.

Our resentment also festers because it leads to resentment towards us from others. As we saw in Gwen's case, her bitterness repelled her family members and the nursing staff who were looking after her. It led them to feel resentful towards her, which no doubt again confirmed and reinforced her view that the world was against her.

Going back to the work I did with the oncology professor discussed in Chapter 1, he was interested in taking up research to explore the impact of gratitude not only on patients but also on their carers. He had observed that, with uncanny frequency, disrespect and negativity from resentful patients adversely affected those who cared for them. They would not only avoid or take shortcuts in caring for these patients but, over time, would also mentally and emotionally suffer from the constant berating and complaints from them. Eventually the caregivers became resentful towards those patients who treated them badly, and then they were less caring towards all their other patients. The professor speculated that this vicious cycle was very likely to be playing a significant role in the high rates of burnout among doctors and nurses when they worked with many resentful patients. In fact, studies on resentment in the context of caregiving have indicated that carers who resent having to care for their older relatives are prone to anxiety and depression.[7, 8]

This was of great concern to the professor, because he has a particular interest in the quality of end-of-life care for his patients. He could see that those who were grateful were much easier to care for, which in turn seemed to have a more positive impact on their quality of life.[9]

## Resentment is the opposite of gratitude

Another way to understand resentment is to see it in terms of its opposite – gratitude. Again, a telling place to see this play out is in any relationship in which you can't contemplate expressing any gratitude at all. For example, you might avoid picking up the phone or writing an email to your friend to thank them for the lovely dinner they cooked, because underneath you are hurt by feeling belittled by them on a previous occasion.

Philosopher Robert Roberts' analysis of the concepts of gratitude and resentment shows that they are mirror opposites of each other – completely opposite states or ways of being.[10] This doesn't mean that we don't have both gratitude and resentment as part of who we are. We can't have functioning relationships without some gratitude, and most of us are rarely totally free of resentment. What it does mean is that if we are wanting to be genuinely grateful to someone, we can't be resentful towards them at the same time. So, if we want to express gratitude to someone, we first need to address any resentment we have towards them.

You might be able to see this more clearly if you think about the difference in your relationship with someone it's easy to feel gratitude for and with someone it's not because there's too much resentment. When you are in a grateful relationship with someone, you feel like you want to be around them all the time. It's easy to connect with them, to notice and celebrate their good points, and to acknowledge how important the relationship is. On the other hand, when you are resentful, you do your best to avoid the person either physically or emotionally. Even hearing their name can make you bristle or change your mood.

While resentment isolates people from one another, gratitude brings them into a closer relationship, as they think about what they have received and how they can give back. Resentment alienates, but gratitude brings warmth, acceptance, joy and love to relationships. Resentment also drains our energy as we ruminate on what we feel has been taken away from us, whereas gratitude energises us and opens us up not only to what we receive but also to how we can give back. While resentment undermines and destroys relationships, gratitude builds and sustains relationships.

In a way, *both* gratitude and resentment arise out of a cycle of giving and receiving and gift. Gratitude acknowledges what you've received from another and motivates you to give back in some way. Resentment comes with a sense of injustice and entitlement, a feeling that you should have been given something but did not receive it, or that what you were given was hurtful.

With resentment, there is the feeling that others have benefited at our expense. The person who we feel has injured or disappointed us has gained and we have lost. This is why Gwen couldn't let go of her resentment: it was a way of holding on to a sense of power over the situation. With gratitude, everyone wins. When we give, we receive, and we feel good, often leading us to actively look for how we can benefit others.

Both gratitude and resentment also have a 'binding' characteristic. As Robert Roberts suggests: 'gratitude tends to bind us together in relationships of friendly and affectionate reciprocity, whereas resentment tends to repel us from one another, or to bind us in relationships of bitter and hostile reciprocity'.[11] As we explored, resentment resists being able to forgive because it binds us to the hurtful event, keeping it alive in us in painful ways.

## Gratitude as a practice

With all that we have learned about gratitude and resentment so far, you might feel a little overwhelmed or have a sense of it all being too hard, or to want to seek out relationships where it's easy to be grateful. In fact, once you are more in touch with your resentment, gratitude to a person you feel has wronged you might seem even more difficult than you originally envisioned. Logic tells you that as they are the one who has hurt you, it's they who should be doing this work, not you. You therefore need to find ways of accessing gratitude in the midst of your resentment, especially when it's the last thing you feel like doing.

Moving from resentment towards gratitude won't be something that you will just think of doing automatically. In fact, you will quite possibly think of a whole lot of reasons why you don't want to do it, or will be tempted to procrastinate and do other things that make you feel more comfortable. My aim is to show you how to do it so that it doesn't feel daunting, and so that you can confidently embrace gratitude in ways that feel comfortable for you, thereby starting to untangle your ball of string.

This can be achieved if we deepen our concept of what gratitude is. So far, we have explored the notion of deep gratitude, which is a purposeful action that arises from a feeling of gratefulness or out of recognition that we have received something from someone, and we are motivated to return our thanks in some way. When we try to be grateful in the midst of resentment, it's helpful to remember that gratitude is an action we practise, rather than a spontaneous positive feeling or something we can instantly 'do'.[12, 13, 14]

Just like learning how to play a musical instrument, for instance, it's not a one-off action that needs to be perfect the first time we try. The notion of 'practice' encourages us to consider that we are 'trying out' something in order to become more skilled. There's no room for perfectionism or judging ourselves. We certainly can't start by considering ourselves to be experts. The most important thing is that we are trying. So, when we are practising gratitude, we recognise that this is a work in progress, and one that we need to return to often so that we can get a little closer to our goal each time. Just as, if you are learning the violin, you need to practise, whether or not you feel like it at the time. You don't wait for the right conditions to occur. Otherwise, you wouldn't make any progress.

For us to succeed, we need to set realistic goals. Rather than trying to express gratitude to everyone around us, or to all those about whom we feel resentful, it would be wise to choose one or two people or situations and work steadily and consistently on developing our gratitude with these. It's also important that we start with those that are a little out of our comfort zone, but not too much. In this way, we choose a gratitude practice that stretches us a little, but not to the point of causing even more resentment.

For example, you might choose a person at work who has ignored your many requests to keep the noise down, leaving you feeling disrespected and resentful. This would be far more achievable than choosing someone who you feel has deeply hurt you, or someone you have deeply resented for a long period of time. The awareness, skills and confidence you gain from this one practice will make it easier to apply them in harder situations.

Your first goal might be to write down why you feel resentful. As we have explored in this chapter, identifying your resentment is a very powerful act because it brings to light what has been hidden, and you are able to act with greater consciousness about what is really going on. A next step, if you are able, might be to try to acknowledge your part in the situation instead of putting the blame totally on the other person. Another way forward might be to start looking for what you are grateful for in this person, or to look at their good points. Rather than being one-off actions, we make these into gratitude practices by taking the time to reflect and come back to them if we need to. Each time we do this, the untangling can continue.

When we are practising gratitude, it's important to feel that this is affirming who we are rather than diminishing us. Although it may not feel natural, at least we need to feel better about ourselves in the process. An advantage of thinking about gratitude as a practice is that it gives us the chance to try something out and work out if it feels authentic and real to us. Most importantly, we can gauge whether it is causing us to feel stressed and therefore beyond our reach at that point in time.

As we explored in Chapter 1, we practise gratitude so that we can change ourselves rather than the other person. It's crucial to keep this at the forefront of our minds, especially when we are practising gratitude in the midst of resentment. Our shock and sense of the injustice of the situation would naturally have us wanting the other person to realise the error of their ways and apologise. This is why it's important to remember that we are *practising* gratitude: it takes a lot of conscious effort on our part to focus on what *we* are doing, on how *we* are changing and growing and moving past our resentment, regardless of what is going on with the other person.

Because gratitude and resentment are direct opposites of each other, each time we make a move out of our resentment, we are moving towards gratitude. Therefore, each of these actions is a gratitude practice in itself. I therefore invite you to think about gratitude not simply as a warm expression of thanks but as a proactive step you take to address your resentment.

## Resentment shows us what matters

As discussed, what resentment shows us most clearly is that the people in our lives matter. Their reactions to us matter, and our sense of justice around these reactions matters. They matter so deeply that they dominate most of the decisions we make about the relationships in our lives. We have our radars up for those who are likely to hurt us, and we put in place a range of protective behaviours to keep those we feel have hurt us – or might do so – at bay.

Our goal here is to see where gratitude and resentment dwell in different areas of our lives, as then we will be able to see them more clearly in each other's light. Through a greater understanding of resentment, we are able to identify feelings and reactions that have remained hidden for years. We should never underestimate the power of the courageous act of identifying where we have resentment and how it plays out in our lives. Such self-knowledge is golden. It enables us to be kinder both to ourselves and to others.

In this chapter, we have explored the importance of identifying resentment so that we can allow gratitude to have a stronger force in our lives. In Chapters 3 and 4, we will further investigate the nature of resentment by exploring its underlying causes, and the role that gratitude can play in addressing these.

# Characteristics of resentment

- ❖ Often hidden deep in the subconscious

- ❖ Sometimes hard to recognise in ourselves

- ❖ Needs to be identified before it can be acted upon proactively

- ❖ Thrives where there is no gratitude

- ❖ Can lead to feeling like a victim and blaming another

- ❖ Held onto out of a sense of injustice

- ❖ Initiated by a shock that causes it to stay lodged

- ❖ Can be all-consuming and make it difficult to focus on other things

- ❖ Leads us to ruminate over the painful event

- ❖ Lingers over time

- ❖ Makes us feel powerless in choosing our state

- ❖ Can generate other resentments

- ❖ Cancels out gratitude and memory of the good in another

- ❖ Often manifests as backbiting, gossiping, cynicism or ridicule

- ❖ Caused by broken expectations and a sense of being made to feel inferior

# Chapter 3

## Broken expectations

*Underneath the most annoying behaviour is a
frustrated person who is crying out for compassion.*
– Rachel Carson

You may now have a clearer idea about how to identify resentment and the impact it may be having on your everyday life. You may wonder how some of your relationships got so difficult and entangled in the first place. The answer can often lie in understanding the causes of your resentment. In this chapter, we'll explore how one of the most common causes – broken expectations – can lead to feelings of disappointment, betrayal and unfairness, all of which can engender resentment. In Chapter 4, we'll look at the role of gratitude in addressing the resentment that arises from a sense of inferiority, which is usually accompanied by feeling diminished or ridiculed.

## When friends disappoint us

I had the honour of being invited to present a day-long workshop on the role of gratitude to a group of elite athletes soon after they returned from the Rio 2016 Summer Olympics and Paralympics. My friends thought this was quite ironic, as I'm the least sporty person you could meet. I don't play it, I don't watch it, and I'm not particularly interested in it. I therefore felt anxious about how relevant this work would be in a sporting context. I was searching for some common ground, something that would resonate with athletes in the same way as it had with my students at university.

The beginning of the workshop focused on the wonderful benefits of gratitude, as experienced by hundreds of participants who had been part of my research projects. We also looked at the benefits of gratitude as revealed in a multitude of scientific studies. However, it wasn't until we started to discuss ways in which gratitude can be difficult and complex that the group's interest and energy grew. It was here I found my common ground, and again, the question 'How can I be grateful when I feel so resentful?' resonated around the room.

As we were discussing this topic, I noticed that one of the athletes, Jocelyn, looked uneasy. It was hard for her to get the words out, but she managed to say that she had a perfect example of resentment and wanted to share it with us. She then told us about what happened when one of her teammates, a close friend named Alice, didn't make it through the selection process for the Games.

The two of them had been training together for eight years, always with the goal of competing together at their first Olympic Games. Alice was devastated when Jocelyn was selected for the team and she missed out. While feeling elated for herself, Jocelyn also felt grief-stricken and somewhat guilty about this unexpected outcome for Alice. It was something that neither of them had prepared for.

Alice was bitterly disappointed and angry. She struggled with what felt like a very public failure and a sense of inferiority, and this led to her spreading some malicious rumours about Jocelyn. She started backbiting her to several of their mutual friends and other elite athletes and their coaches. When Jocelyn heard about this, she felt shocked and betrayed. All of the gratitude that Jocelyn had originally felt for Alice was now so consumed by her resentment that no matter how much she tried, she couldn't stay away from the negative thoughts that were churning around in her head.

I don't think I will ever forget the moment when she shared the next part of her story. Jocelyn admitted to us all that she had carried these feelings of resentment right into the finals of the Olympics.

Even though all Jocelyn's dreams had come true – not only had she made it to the Olympic Games but here she was in the finals, with the whole of her country cheering her on – at that significant and crucial moment, when she needed to be at her most focused, Jocelyn confessed to us that all she could think about was the disappointment over what she saw as her betrayal by Alice. Her feelings of resentment robbed her of the joy of the pivotal experience she had worked so hard for.

Jocelyn won a silver medal in her event. It was a great achievement, but she believed that she would have had a greater chance of winning gold if she had known how to stop her resentment from taking such a hold over her. She realised in our workshop that if she could have recognised it for what it was, and learned how to work through it, the outcome for her might have been different. Here Jocelyn was, months later, still suffering because there was a part of her that was blaming Alice for the fact that she didn't win gold.

Jocelyn had been coached in the state-of-the-art strategies of focused attention and positive mindset. She'd been practising these strategies for years. Yet when it came to the moment when it really counted, the tug of her resentment was too strong for them to be effective.

## Missing out on selection

The other athletes in the room nodded in agreement as Jocelyn related her experience. They spoke of it being a common occurrence for them too, particularly at times of selection for competitions. With passion, they shared stories of massive fallouts with their teammates and relationships lost because resentments were not addressed. They also told tales of how their physical and mental wellbeing had been negatively affected. Some of their friends had even left their sport entirely, totally devastated.

Although they empathised with Jocelyn about the inappropriate ways in which Alice reacted, they were also seeing it from Alice's perspective. They shared stories of the immense disappointment they felt after training hard at dawn and then again before dusk, nearly every day of the year, year after year. To then miss out on selection for a major competition was heartbreaking and something that was very hard to come back from, particularly when they were so young.

You may have experienced something similar in your life, where you have poured your heart and soul into a goal for years only to be bitterly disappointed when it didn't turn out as you expected. Not being selected for a position at work is a classic example of this. It's common to struggle with the sense of injustice if you feel that all your efforts in your role up to that point weren't acknowledged in the way you expected.

We may also experience this disappointment and ensuing resentment as parents. From the time of conception, it's only natural for us to have big plans for our children. We might sacrifice a lot so that they can achieve their potential. When they miss out on achieving the goals we wanted for them, or when things don't turn out according to how we expect, especially if they take what we think is a rather destructive path, it's hard not to feel resentful.

## The weightiness of expectations

Another point struck me in the stories told by the athletes. We might have an image of sportspeople as heroic figures who are highly competitive, focused and unstoppable. Yet at the core of who they are – at the core of who we all are – is a human being. Part of being human is that we are always *in relationship* with others. No matter how much we might focus on individual pursuits and isolate ourselves to achieve our goals, when our relationships cause us pain that we can't let go of, it eats into our being and affects every aspect of our lives.

Nearly all relationships – both personal and professional – are built on expectations. In some cases, they are built on the values or ethics we think we share with others. Often, they are established around what we feel people should and shouldn't do, or how they should or shouldn't behave in their role, according to various unwritten agreements. For example, in contemporary Australian culture, we have an expectation that parents should treat their children equally and not have favourites. We also expect employers to follow due process when offering a promotion and not favour one employee over another. As was the case with Gwen in Chapter 2, we also have an expectation that our wedded partner will stay with us 'till death us do part'.

In an ideal world, our expectations would be clearly communicated and revisited often for further clarity and assurance, and we would check in to see whether we want an agreement to change. However, many of us haven't been taught this fine art of communication and feel awkward when approaching significant people in our lives to discuss agreements or expectations. How do we raise the topic without it seeming like we don't trust the other person? How do we do so without making it a big deal or too formal?

It's important to note that we often arrive at these expectations without necessarily including the other person in our thinking. We just expect them to agree, based on the strength of the bond, the assumption that cultural norms are shared, or past experience – we project onto them what we would like to happen and imagine that they are on the same page. In my opinion, this is a significant reason why we have so much conflict in our relationships, and why too many of our relationships are tainted by resentment.

The relationship between Jocelyn and Alice was based on a whole string of expectations. As best friends, they expected mutual respect irrespective of selection. They expected that this mutual respect would prevent either one from backbiting or gossiping about the other. They expected that the closeness they felt would remain, regardless of the selection outcome. They both expected maturity and self-management in whatever situation arose.

Jocelyn also had high expectations of her own capacity to deal with the situation, which in turn led to self-resentment (a topic covered in

Chapter 6). Before our workshop, she hadn't talked to anyone about her pain. She felt ashamed that she wasn't able to put it aside and that it was affecting her so badly. She felt that to admit otherwise to her coaches would be seen as a weakness. It was too risky in case she was judged incapable of performing at her best. Given all the investment the sporting organisation had made in preparing their athletes to be focused, Jocelyn also felt she was a failure in not being able to rise above her feelings.

Many of the athletes said that they were greatly relieved to finally have some language to talk about this lingering feeling of resentment they had been unable to let go of. They also found solace in the fact that they were not alone.

In light of these revelations, I was invited to give presentations and workshops to coaches of elite athletes. I was given permission to share the story of Jocelyn and Alice. A common refrain from those subsequent workshops was that the coaches themselves had not had the language to describe this dynamic either. They spoke of the time when they were elite athletes themselves and had been devastated about not being selected for a competition. They shared the accompanying shame and feeling of public humiliation. For many in the room, the transition from athlete to coach had been marked by deep bitterness about non-selection, as they felt things had not been handled well.

Some of them even admitted that their coaching lacked joy because they could not let go of their resentment. They reported that through these gratitude workshops they were now becoming conscious of how much this had hardened them in their relationships with the athletes. As their disappointment and ensuing resentment had not been addressed by their coaches, they didn't have any precedent or skills for managing their athletes' wellbeing when they missed out on selection. Rather, they felt they needed to 'toughen them up' so they could deal with the blows that were 'inevitable' if their expectations were not met.

An important question, and one that this sporting organisation began pondering deeply, was: when should the training around resentment and gratitude take place?

Resentment arising from broken expectations is everywhere. In every school and university context where I have presented this work, there has been common agreement among educators that resentment is rife among students.

Students are often judged by their teachers as having a sense of entitlement. This is typically how they explain the rise in what they perceive as disengagement and disrespectful behaviour. I believe that the real cause is much deeper, however: it's that they have high expectations of their teachers or their educational institution and are disappointed and shocked when they feel that these are not met. Resentment can also arise from disappointment if students feel let down by their parents, other family members, peers or governments past and present, and they bring this resentment into their classroom.

In the school context, resentment can also be fuelled by parents if they join with their children to complain about the ineffective or 'mean' teacher, or the incompetent institution. Parents' resentment over broken expectations feeds their children's resentment, and vice versa.

In my experience, many students don't know how to manage resentment arising from their broken expectations, and this negatively affects their learning in profound ways. As mentioned in the introduction – and it's worth repeating – students have not been educated in how to overcome their resentment, and this diminishes their ability to be present in their learning.

## Adopting a wiser lens

As explored in Chapter 2, resentment is an emotion connected to our sense of justice. Our expectations are usually deeply entrenched within our values – how we think the world should operate, how relationships should work and how people should behave. So, when our expectations are not met, something deep inside our moral framework, or indeed in our hearts, gets broken. We can become totally disorientated by the shock of things not being as we believe they should be. We keep processing it in our heads, trying to make sense of it all, to dislodge the wrongness and make it better somehow, but this usually makes it worse and leads us to project our pain onto the one who we feel has wronged us.

Jocelyn said that she had not contacted Alice since she first heard of the rumours that Alice had been spreading. She didn't receive any congratulations from Alice once she had made it to the final, or when she won a silver medal. At this point, Jocelyn couldn't imagine how they could be friends again.

When feeling resentful, it often doesn't take much to hurl out those who break our expectations into the 'no friend', 'can't be trusted' zone – the outer circle. We take refuge in the relationships we believe will never let us down. We may well settle for those that don't challenge us or help us grow, because at least there is less risk of being hurt. We might settle for a kind of mediocrity in our relationships with our friends, in our workplace or even with our partner, so that we feel safe.

Some respond to their resentment by declaring that they just won't have any expectations anymore. Then no one gets hurt, and there's no disappointment. This is often touted as a sign of wisdom. You've probably come across sayings like: 'If you expect nothing from anybody, you are never disappointed,' or: 'Peace begins when expectations end.'

Others say that if we lower our expectations, it's easier to be grateful, because we are pleasantly surprised when someone exceeds them. The argument also goes that because we're less likely to be disappointed if we have low expectations, we are less likely to become resentful. As author Isaac Asimov put it, 'People who don't expect justice don't have to suffer disappointment.'

Perhaps this could be sage advice with regard to life events that are out of our control, but I believe that we can seek a deeper wisdom when we apply it to our relationships with others. In some sense, giving up or lowering our expectations might give us a kind of peace, but in another, it can lead to numbness, indifference and a reduced opportunity for healthy and nourishing connections with others. Without high expectations, we may well lose our bearings. It's our expectations that help define us and help us make decisions about what we believe to be right and wrong in the world.

Could we apply a wiser lens here? The problem doesn't necessarily lie in the expectations. It lies in what we do with them, especially if they're unspoken, particularly rigid, or if we lack the skills or confidence to talk about them with others and negotiate mutual agreements. A wiser approach would be to hold high expectations *and* not be attached to the outcome. We keep our standards regarding how we want to be treated, for example, but we don't have the emotional attachment to things turning out exactly as we expect. This takes a good deal of maturity. However, the more we can practise acceptance by being detached from particular outcomes, the less resentful we will be.

Gratitude can help with this acceptance process, and indeed acceptance is one of the pillars of gratitude. Gratitude orientates us to look for the learning in adversity and to therefore take disappointment as an opportunity to grow and change. It helps us to remember the good, so that we are able to focus on what we have rather than what we don't have, or, in this case, where others or life let us down. A grateful state also gives us the resilience or buoyancy we need to be able to accept disappointment.

Choosing to cultivate gratitude as a way of working through our resentments doesn't mean that we accept the status quo if our expectations are not met. It just means that we are more conscious of what we value in the other person and are able to remember all we have received in the relationship. We are less likely to cast the other person aside if they disappoint us, because gratitude helps remind us of the good and gives us another way of looking at the situation.

## Moving to compassion

Such wisdom is easier to access when we value the relationship as much as we value our own goals or achieving our pursuits. This is fine if we aren't stressed, overworked or time-poor, but we often are. Even if we do value our relationships, just being able to survive in a competitive, performance-driven world can make us put them second. The problem is that putting tasks above people gives rise to what philosopher Martin Buber describes as an 'I–It' relationship, where we treat people as means to our own ends. This is in contrast to an 'I–Thou' relationship, where we are connecting with another as an end in itself, because they matter and the relationship matters.[1]

A way to start to untangle some of our ball of string is to cultivate our compassion for another, to consciously keep an I–Thou relationship with them. It's when we see and value them as a person, and accept them with all their frailties and vulnerability, that we are able to withstand disappointment if our expectations are not met. We are able to apply the deep wisdom of Rachel Carson that I quoted at the beginning of this chapter: 'Underneath the most annoying behaviour is a frustrated person who is crying out for compassion.'[2] If we put ourselves in the shoes of another and seek to understand the situation from their perspective, we can gain insights that help lessen the pain of broken expectations.

It's completely understandable that it was initially impossible for Jocelyn to respond with gratitude to her pre-Olympic friendship with Alice. After our workshop, however, she was able to speak to her coach Vlad about what she'd realised about the resentment she felt towards Alice. Because Vlad was Alice's coach as well, he was able to explain to Jocelyn how painful the experience of not being selected had been for her. Vlad reminded Jocelyn that Alice was a perfectionist, and so her non-selection brought public shame that she had never recovered from. He told her that on paper, perhaps, Alice looked like a surer candidate for selection than Jocelyn, as she'd had more wins in certain competitions. Jocelyn had been so consumed by her resentment that she had forgotten that it would have been a very close call for the selection committee, and in fact she was fortunate to have been chosen instead of Alice. Obsessed by her thoughts about how she felt Alice had betrayed their friendship, she hadn't been able to put herself in Alice's shoes.

Jocelyn was also moved by Vlad's account of the resentment he felt from his own experience of not being selected for a major international event. Jocelyn was very close to Vlad, as she had worked with him for over a decade, but she had never known how hard it had been for him to deal with his resentment. Although Jocelyn gained some comfort from the stories shared at our workshop, it was only when Vlad talked of his own dysfunctional behaviour that stemmed from resentment – which included backbiting his fellow competitors and storming out of crucial team meetings – that Jocelyn was able to see that this behaviour was common, even among people she idolised.

Through these experiences, Jocelyn was able to free herself from the grip of resentment and feel more compassionate towards Alice. She could also see that her resentment had prevented her from seeing how difficult it would have been for Alice *not* to react in the way she did. Jocelyn started to realise that her expectations of their friendship were perhaps unrealistic, particularly because they were never clearly communicated or mutually agreed upon.

Vlad also admitted that the antagonism between Alice and Jocelyn could have been lessened if he had facilitated better communication regarding their expectations at the time of selection. He learned a great deal from Jocelyn's courageous sharing of her resentment with him. It helped him become more conscious of his own resentment, and he was a better coach for it.

Jocelyn could have chosen to trust no one, and certainly to never trust Alice again. Instead, her new gratitude practices of identifying her resentment, growing her compassion and putting herself in the shoes of another enabled Jocelyn to contact Alice and apologise for her part in the conflict.

Jocelyn's increased capacity for compassion didn't make Alice's actions right and Jocelyn's reactions wrong, but it was important for her to communicate how upset she'd been and how Alice's actions had negatively impacted upon her. She needed to find a healthy balance between compassion towards Alice and holding on to what was true for her. In resolving conflict, both parties need to stand strong and learn from each other. What Jocelyn's newfound compassion gave her, though, was a more conciliatory entry point for this conversation and a standpoint where she wanted to hear Alice's side of the story.

With time, Jocelyn was able to see that it was not a natural part of Alice's character to hurt her when things didn't turn out the way she wanted. She was able to relegate the hurtful things that happened between them to a particular moment in time, one that is now understood and forgiven by both of them.

## Growing our empathy through gratitude

Our resentment can make us incapable of empathy, of looking at the situation from another's perspective or putting ourselves in their shoes. Resentment can become so all-consuming that it keeps us stuck in a binary position: we are right and they are wrong; we are good and they are bad. Then it becomes all about our pain, and there is no place to consider the other. We can't find any empathy towards someone if we are consumed by the injustice they have committed and the hurt we feel they have caused us.

This can be particularly prevalent in single-minded pursuits. One of the leading thinkers in the world of empathy, Simon Baron-Cohen, points to Buber's work to explain that people with 'zero degrees of empathy' turn people into objects, where 'there is no Thou' visible. While we might think that this state of zero empathy is the signature of sociopaths or psychopaths, Baron-Cohen alerts us to the fact that 'when a person is solely focused on the pursuit of their own interests, they have all the potential to be unempathic'.[3]

He goes on to say, 'Interestingly, in this state of single-minded pursuit of one's own goals, one's project might even have a positive focus: helping people, for example. But even if a person's project is positive, worthy and valuable, if it is single-minded, it is by definition, unempathic.'[4] In my own context, these words helped me make sense of what happens to many academics, and why, in my humble opinion, many university communities are floundering under the weight of resentment. Our obsession with our research (a vital part of an academic's career) can cause us to push relationships aside, giving gratitude very little space to live and breathe because those relationships are considered irrelevant.

Our self-absorption can be further fuelled by resentment. One of the characteristics of resentment is that it tends to make us turn inward and become self-oriented. The pain we feel from disappointment about another can be all-consuming. However, if we can find a way to practise gratitude more frequently and authentically, the opposite happens. It moves us out of self-absorption into connectedness with another person. The experience of gratitude helps us to make relationships more important than the task at hand. It reminds us of all that we have received from another, and thus makes us more connected to them.

Gratitude therefore creates the conditions in which empathy can grow. By accepting the invitation to look at what we have been given, we can become more *for-giving*. Our gratitude has the power to turn our attention from inward to outward.

The move towards gratitude is inherently a call to give priority to the relationship as an end in itself, not to serve our needs. When we practise gratitude, we grow our sense of relatedness, of indebtedness, of interdependence – and see that we are all connected. This does not mean we don't feel anger, hurt or frustration. But if we're centred in gratitude, these emotions are less likely to develop into resentment, and we're less likely to get stuck, to have 'hard feelings' or to bear a grudge.

## The giving and receiving circle of gratitude

This orientation towards what we have been given rather than what we feel the other has taken away from us can be facilitated by a deeper understanding of various dimensions of gratitude. So, there are really four elements that make up gratitude – a giver, a receiver, a gift, and the 'attitudes of the giver and recipient towards one another'.[5] Gratitude flows through the attitude we bring to a situation, by consciously and purposefully looking for gifts we receive from others, even those who hurt us.

These elements also distinguish gratitude from other kinds of action that are commonly bundled together with gratitude, such as praise, positive feedback, kindness, good manners, applause and positive acknowledgment. They may be ways in which gratitude is expressed, but if they are not expressed with the intention of giving because of an awareness of what we have received, they are not the same as acts of gratitude.

My research shows that many people are far better at expressing gratitude than receiving it from others. To be on the receiving end of another's gratitude can feel awkward – especially when we have grown up in environments where gratitude is rarely expressed. We might see our personality as one that is not openly effusive when receiving acknowledgment from another. There can be a shying away through a sense of obligation that the gratitude might imply, a feeling that we are now indebted to return the thanks offered or to behave in the same way as the demonstratively grateful person.

When we feel resentful, it can be impossible to take in another's gratitude. In fact, we might repel it. This can plant a seed of resentment in the other person, especially if they want to express gratitude as a way of breaking the ice or connecting with us.

Likewise, it doesn't take much for us to feel awkward or disappointed when the recipient of our gratitude shuts us down, or acts suspicious, embarrassed or even offended. For example, the elite athletes I spoke to told me that one of the biggest challenges in expressing gratitude to their coaches was that they didn't know how it would be received by them. Would it be seen as attempting to curry favour for selection, or would it be seen as unnecessary given they were just doing their job? They reported that some coaches had ridiculed them or scoffed at their expressions of gratitude. This stopped the athletes, from thanking them. In this lay the beginnings of resentment in the athletes, who were not able to be themselves in expressing what came naturally to them, and in the coaches who felt awkward and embarrassed by the athletes' gratitude.

A recent experience for me highlighted the importance of the receiver in the dynamic of giving and receiving. A few months into a very painful bout of shingles, my immune system was so low that I contracted cellulitis. This led me to being rushed into the emergency department of a local hospital after a sleepless night of acute pain and nausea. The most touching moment of that experience was when a nurse came and asked me if I was okay and if she could make me a cup of tea. I cried because of her kindness, her deeply caring voice and manner. I had been observing the staff for a few hours, and most looked exhausted, including this nurse.

On leaving the hospital, I really wanted to thank this nurse. I caught a glimpse of her as I was walking out and thought that she recognised me. I asked at the reception desk if I could thank her or if my thanks could be passed on, but was told that they 'don't do that kind of thing here – it's part of our job'. I couldn't help but wonder at that moment how much those staff were missing out on the nourishment that sincere gratitude from their patients could give them, if only the system and they themselves were open to it. As a patient I felt stultified, as my immense gratitude had nowhere to go.

There was no way to complete the circle, except perhaps to pass it on to someone else in need of a 'cuppa' at some time in the future. But in this instance, it didn't feel like the same thing. The wheel of giving and receiving was not able to turn. What's more, the systems and culture that are the context to our relationships play a big part in determining the extent to which the elements of gratitude are able to circulate. As with the example of the sporting organisation, if they wanted to grow a culture in which gratitude thrives and resentment isn't able to fester, it would be important to educate all parties to become better at both giving *and* receiving gratitude. The best place to start is to observe and learn from someone who is really good at receiving gratitude.

This is also central to allowing gratitude to increase our empathy and compassion. The better we are at receiving gratitude, the more we can feel a deep connection with another, understand them more fully and help them to feel valued by us. We stop and take note of their efforts in appreciating the relationship. Again, this is particularly important in relationships marked by resentment.

\* \* \*

In this chapter we have explored the ways in which gratitude is destroyed by the resentment arising from broken expectations. We've also seen how gratitude has an important part to play in helping us value relationships more than tasks or our single-minded pursuits, and in helping us put ourselves in another's shoes so that we have a greater understanding of why people make the choices they do. When we are trying to untangle some of our difficult relationships, a helpful place to start is identifying if our resentment has been caused by broken expectations, and to adopt the gratitude practices of growing our compassion and our empathy and becoming better at both giving and receiving gratitude.

In the next chapter, we will delve further into how gratitude can assist us to identify our resentment by looking at another significant underlying cause: being made to feel inferior.

# Chapter 4

## A sense of inferiority

*There is in human beings a powerful longing to be recognised.*
– Margaret Visser

### Sent out to pasture

Madeline was coming to the end of an illustrious career in human resources within a large communications organisation. Her position for the past decade had been team leader of innovative practice across all the organisation's branches. She was very experienced in her role, with master's-level qualifications, and had presented state-of-the-art communication strategies in many parts of the country. She'd gained well-earned respect and a reputation nationwide for her skills and abilities. She had won awards, given keynote addresses, developed training modules and been invited to sit on a number of boards.

Having had the good fortune to work with highly collaborative teams over her long career, Madeline was perplexed when she encountered some alienating types of behaviour from the most recent crop of team leaders, who had been selected by the new general manager of the organisation. She couldn't put her finger on it, and nothing was explicitly said to her, but a number of incidents led her to feel that she was being treated with some disdain by some of the other leaders, as well as by the general manager. This grew worse as the months rolled on.

Just before this started to happen, Madeline had returned from a two-week course on a new form of coaching at a prestigious training institute overseas. It had built on her already considerable expertise, and so now she naturally assumed that her skills would be called upon after her return to lead a new rollout of this program across the organisation. However, this role was given to another of the team leaders, who had much less experience and knowledge, even though it was Madeline who had already established much of the groundwork. At the weekly meetings where this program was discussed, Madeline wasn't consulted at all, nor was she asked to contribute any of the strategies she had learned at the overseas course. She felt marginalised and invisible and was starting to develop a sense of inferiority she'd never experienced before.

This led Madeline to feel a little paranoid. After all, no one was saying anything directly to her about why she was being treated differently. She observed that others in the team were given information but she wasn't. Things were being discussed in meetings that she wasn't invited to. All of a sudden, people who she thought were close colleagues seemed to be avoiding her and were not asking her to join them for lunch. She wondered what she had done wrong. She kept going over the events of the past few months to try to figure out if she had said or done something to offend the manager or anyone else.

Madeline finally started to put a few pieces of the jigsaw together, and it slowly dawned on her that as she was nearing retirement, the new general manager was trying to push her out more quickly than she was choosing to go. It appeared as if the other team leaders were part of a new regime and saw themselves as the new look of the organisation. She was being made to feel that she was no longer needed, no longer wanted and definitely in the way. The shock of this realisation and the humiliating treatment she was experiencing made Madeline feel very resentful. She could no longer think clearly, and this fed into her growing sense of inadequacy.

Eventually Madeline lost her sense of worth and usefulness in the workplace. She had a constant feeling of anxiety, a tightness in the gut. She dreaded going to work and lost a lot of sleep, tossing and turning at night, ruminating on the injustice of it all. What's worse, she was also beating herself up for not being stronger and rising above the sense of humiliation, and was shocked at how much it had rocked her. Madeline had endured all kinds of adversity, but this situation somehow destabilised her more than any other.

## Being made to feel inferior

In Warren TenHouten's words: 'Resentment arises when one is placed in an inferior position, and where harmful treatment is undeserved, unfair, insulting, or injurious.'[1]

Madeline's sense of feeling inferior was brought about by conditions that are common in many workplaces today. In fact, a 2021 World Health Organization report on ageism found that, globally, one in two people are guilty of it. The report also showed how ageism reduces older people's quality of life, increases their social isolation and loneliness, and can lead to poorer physical and mental health.[2]

How ageism plays out in workplaces might well make us feel stonewalled, excluded from collegial friendships or deliberately kept in the dark about important matters. For the sake of a new project, task or innovation, our contribution can be sidelined if no longer deemed necessary. New ways of doing things are often considered the territory of new blood, young blood, and there is often no time for kindness or empathy towards those who aren't invited along for the ride. The people who are leading the restructure or new project are often too task-focused or performance-oriented to notice that their actions are leaving others feeling diminished and disillusioned. Trust diminishes; paranoia flourishes; resentment festers.

One of the most natural expectations we have of others is that they will treat us fairly and equitably. As we saw in Madeline's case, the realisation that we are not being treated as equal, or that we are judged to be inferior, can totally disorientate us. It can shatter how we see ourselves in the world and shake us to the core. We need to go over and over the situation to try to regain our sense of self and our sense of who we are in the world, and to maintain our sanity. Resentment becomes our way to gain back power and reassert our dignity, as we talk about the injustice of it all to anyone who will listen. Or, as politics academic Michael Ure states, 'The motive of resentment is... restoration of wounded honor or recognition – respect.'[3]

Other common situations where we are resentful because of this feeling of inferiority include being the brunt of other people's jokes – or worse, their prejudices; when a sibling receives preferential treatment from parents; betrayal by a partner who gives their heart to

someone else; and, as we saw in the last chapter, whe'
is selected for the team over us. As this is often done in ५.
way, the humiliation is amplified and can seem inescapable.

It also doesn't take much for us to feel inferior in the presence of
someone who has power over us. They may not be intending to use
this power to make us feel inferior, but they can readily cause offence
and hurt with off-hand remarks or by failing to acknowledge us. This
increases our sense of inferiority.

We see this play out sometimes in the case of a child's resentment.
It's often difficult for parents to navigate the natural power imbalance
in the parent–child relationship in a conscious way. Just by virtue of
being a parent, we feel we have authority over what our children can
and can't do. Sometimes a child's angry response is the only way they
can find to make themselves feel less inferior, more powerful and in
control. They need to gain a sense of power or self-worth, and when
they can't they feel resentful. We have not consciously taken this away
from them, but this is often what it feels like for our children.

They may be living in a world where many other things are
contributing to them feeling inferior – bullying among their peers,
discomfort with their body image or a sense of failure at school. These
situations can lead to an overall feeling of losing control and losing
their stable place in the world.

## Reconnaissance

So, what could be done for Madeline to be able to address her
resentment? Actually, despite the humiliation she felt at her
workplace, there was a kernel of salvation: Madeline was still running
a program with a group of facilitators in a regional part of the state

and continued to meet with them face-to face every fortnight. It was here that she was reminded that she still had something valuable to offer; she felt respected and recognised. Many of the facilitators would thank her for her contribution or talk about how much they appreciated her insights.

However, the team leaders and her manager weren't at all aware of the amazing difference this program was making to staff in the regional branch and the significant part Madeline was playing in bringing about this productive change. Madeline kept it secret, feeling that by doing so, she was protecting a part of her dignity and self-respect that could not be taken away from her.

When she arrived for the afternoon meeting, one of the facilitators would often have baked a cake and others would fuss over Madeline, offering her a cup of tea and thanking her for travelling so far to be with them. She bathed in their gentle appreciation. She felt endorsed, successful and welcomed. The efforts they made to put their other work aside and be together, and the delight they took in sharing their ideas with Madeline, touched her greatly.

It was this team's acknowledgment of her and their recognition of her value, as well as the success of the program, that kept Madeline sane. The safety and trust she felt among this group of people was in stark and painful contrast to the atmosphere of competitive judgment and contempt she experienced in her main office. Indeed, finding psychological safety in the workplace is increasingly hard these days, exacerbating the conditions in which resentment can grow.

Madeline's sense of inferiority would have been much worse if she didn't have this reprieve. The recognition and appreciation she received from this team gave her the resilience and sense of self she needed in order to be able to look at what was happening to her more objectively. It offered her a different choice about how she was going to respond.

What this group of facilitators gave to Madeline, even though they weren't aware of it, can be seen through the lens of the French word for gratitude: *reconnaissance*. The origin of the word is the Old French *reconoistre*: 'to recognise'. When we express gratitude by recognising the value or goodness in a person and affirming their worth, we are enacting *reconnaissance*. This concept has been brought to our attention by Margaret Visser in her book *The Gift of Thanks: The Roots and Rituals of Gratitude*. Across all cultures she observes: 'There is in human beings a powerful longing to be recognised.'[4]

Visser sees this need for recognition as a 'fundamental struggle for identity, relationship, and belonging'.[5] If this need is not met, we don't flourish as human beings, and there is a very real threat to our own sense of worthiness. As a fundamental human need, it's no wonder we feel shocked and disoriented when we don't receive it.

Madeline was clearly experiencing *reconnaissance* from her group of facilitators. This didn't take much on their part. It didn't take time or money or an expensive program. Through their greetings, their gestures of appreciation for her and their acknowledgment of what they valued in her contribution, she regained a sense of identity, relationship and belonging that had been stripped from her by the actions of the other group. Madeline experienced an even greater power in this *reconnaissance* because it was offered while she was in the midst of being shattered by the lack of it.

As Margaret Visser tells us, a very important aspect of *reconnaissance* is that we can't give this recognition to ourselves. It needs to come from others. No matter how much Madeline tried to source this sense of being worthwhile from her history or past achievements, she couldn't give this *reconnaissance* to herself. This is one of the reasons why it's crucially important that we show our gratitude to others.

All of this raises another question: if it is a fundamental human need to receive *reconnaissance*, isn't it also a fundamental human need to offer it? Do we lose out if we don't meet this need to recognise people, tell them we value them and express gratitude to them? Does it diminish our integrity, our humanity? I think it does. In the sense of an everyday resentment, we can see this in the context of romantic relationships. We might take our partner for granted and, for example, not greet them when they come home because we are distracted with our own concerns. Over time, not only does the relationship suffer due to the lack of *reconnaissance* we bring to it, but we also suffer personally.

To put it another way, when we recognise what another has given us, it hopefully stirs within us a sense of incompleteness if we don't take action ourselves. Our lack of action resides within us as regret, a quiet guilt, remorse or a sense of something being not quite complete. These feelings are easy to ignore in the midst of our busyness or preoccupations, but this may come at some cost.

When we reflect on this, we may feel a little uneasy about missed opportunities to offer this *reconnaissance* to others in the past. All we can do now is try to do things differently from this moment on. For example, you might like to think of someone in your midst who isn't flourishing, or someone who doesn't have a strong sense of belonging. How might you offer sincere gratitude to them for what you value in them?

## What about bullies?

You may be reading all of this and thinking of people to whom it's just impossible to even contemplate offering this *reconnaissance*, and perhaps there is no more poignant example of this than bullies. It's an understatement to say that we feel inferior when we are being bullied. That's the whole intent of bullying. However, behind every bully is another bully, and behind that bully there is usually a story of put-downs, abuse and trauma. For example, a 2016 UK study on bullying that surveyed 8850 respondents revealed that those who bully others are likely to have experienced stress or trauma themselves in the previous five years.[6] The study also showed that those who have been bullied are twice as likely to go on and bully others. It would follow, therefore, that out of their feeling of inferiority, injustice and broken expectations, the bullies see themselves as standing in justified resentment against the world. Consciousness of this resentment is almost always hidden from them. Bullying is a way of gaining superiority so that they can feel powerful and validated as a person.

Of course, if we are being bullied ourselves, it would seem totally counterintuitive and virtually impossible to even contemplate this situation through the lens of *reconnaissance*. However, if you know of someone who bullies others, it might be worthwhile looking at them through this lens.

If the thing a bully is most craving is affirmation of themselves as a worthwhile human being, and we can think of a deed they've done in the past for which we can thank them, this could help them feel less inferior and perhaps lead to a decrease in the bullying behaviour you've observed in them.

Sometimes we look for complex answers in the face of complex problems, and this can certainly be so in instances such as bullying behaviour. There are volumes of policy documents and resources that give guidance on how best to deal with bullying. My question here is whether or not we have overlooked the simpler and yet more fundamental approach of addressing the bully's sense of inferiority through offering *reconnaissance* – recognition of their inherent value as a human being.

Extending this more widely, we would also be aiming to create workplace and school cultures where *reconnaissance* thrives, so that resentment has less of a chance to take hold. We would be making empathy, compassion, gratitude and respect the norm, and calling out any situations which threaten this. We'd be making it easier for those who are driven by resentment to feel what it's like to receive the opposite.

## Thanking meaningfully

Madeline was moved by the *reconnaissance* offered by the group of facilitators because it was given in a way that was meaningful to her: the cake, the cup of tea, and the thanks and acknowledgment that she had driven a long way. Other gestures would not have been as moving if they had not been attuned to what Madeline needed as a sign of appreciation. As I explored in the introduction, I consciously chose to express my gratitude to my mother by way of a letter. I did this because some of my earliest memories were of her pouring herself into letters to her friends and family when we moved interstate. I also remember her delight at receiving letters and racing to the mailbox at the shrill sound of the postman's whistle. I knew a letter would move her and I consciously chose it as a way of reaching her heart.

A gift is going to be interpreted more clearly as an expression of gratitude if it's consciously chosen, with a clear intention, in terms of its meaning for the other. Deep gratitude is a highly relational act. We need a relationship or connection with the person in order to know how to express gratitude sincerely to them. Even reflecting about how we might meaningfully express gratitude to another person draws us closer to them in our thoughts. As Margaret Visser says '... gratitude causes the receiver to look beyond the gift to the giver... It "opens" the receiver to the person of the other.'[7]

To express gratitude in a meaningful way, it's helpful to recognise that the way we like to show our gratitude, or have it shown to us, may well be different from the way the person we are expressing gratitude to prefers to receive it. If they are from a different culture to our own, this awareness is even more important. Gender and age differences are also significant factors. It's therefore important to attune ourselves to the other person's background, interests and values in order to express gratitude meaningfully.

Additionally, if we don't make an effort to come to know the person first, we can unwittingly sow a seed of resentment. Our expression of gratitude could be interpreted as a mark of disrespect or lack of care. A director of a company may be presented with bottles of white wine at the end of the year as a token of gratitude, but he may feel insulted if he is allergic to wine or doesn't drink. An employee may feel hurt if they receive a gift of thanks in the form of a box of chocolates when they're diabetic.

It's also important to acknowledge that timing and context influence the way another receives our expression of gratitude. This is particularly the case in the context of adversity. If someone is going through a really hard time, we can't necessarily expect them to receive our gratitude in the way that we intend. We may need to delve deeply into how we can still offer them *reconnaissance* in appropriate ways at this time.

Again, the interrelationship between empathy and gratitude is important here. To express *reconnaissance* well, we need to put ourselves in the shoes of the other person to try to see what they would appreciate most. Initially it may be something other than the gratitude we would like to express to them. For example, they might need us to pick up their children or cook them a meal or do whatever is needed so they can have some time alone. Enacting such sensitivity – where we consciously choose the time, the place and the gift so that it is meaningful and appropriate – is already an act of gratitude.

## Attentive listening

When we are left feeling inferior in the way that Madeline experienced, it can shock us to the core. How could this be? How dare they? Aren't they aware of how unfair this is? Don't they know me and how much I have to offer, how much I have given? Again, it's this shock that keeps the resentment lodged solidly in our being and makes it so difficult to move on.

We can take steps to process this shock by talking it over with a trusted friend. There are deliberate choices to be made around which friend to choose and the purpose of talking about our resentment. The more consciousness we bring to these choices, the more objective we can be when we share and process our pain with the other person. It's very important for us to still hold on to our integrity by ensuring our discussion doesn't diminish into a backbiting session.

In this regard, a second kernel of salvation for Madeline came in the form of a trusted colleague. Leah was assisting with the program for the facilitators but came from another interstate office. They would sometimes travel together for the meetings. Madeline was very careful about whom she shared her pain with but felt that she could trust Leah. Leah didn't try to advise or solve the problem. She just gave her whole attention to Madeline in a way that made Madeline feel heard and validated. She helped Madeline to feel okay to sit in the discomfort of the pain she was feeling in order to grow her understanding of what was going on for her. Through this, Madeline felt less isolated. This is important because resentment often festers in situations where we feel alone.

The more Madeline opened up to Leah, the more she could see that her resentment was pervading nearly every area of her life. She could see that it had caused her to give up faith not only in herself but in human nature itself. She could hear herself using words like 'totally horrendous', 'completely unfathomable' and 'grossly unfair'. Always having seen herself as a glass-half-full kind of person, she was shocked and dismayed by how negative she had become.

For Leah to be totally there for Madeline and listen with her whole being was a profound way to express gratitude towards Madeline, to offer *reconnaissance*. If you have experienced what it feels like to be listened to by a person who is completely present with you and for you, who is not judging you and is totally trustworthy, you know what a gift this can be and how affirming it feels.

Listening attentively is all about what we can give, not what we can get from the encounter. It requires genuine presence, truly being with the person. To abandon ourselves for another and put our own ego and agenda aside is one of the most rewarding things to do. It takes humility and empathy. Becoming a good listener is no small feat. Gratitude plays an important role in growing this skill. If we approach our listening with a spirit of gratitude for the opportunity to hear the heart of another, we can feel more connected to them and less distracted by our own thoughts. Most importantly for Madeline, this was the beginning of her untangling process, a way forward at long last.

## Captains of gratitude

To offer *reconnaissance* is an art form that few have mastered. When I ask my workshop participants to think of a person who does this well, many can only nominate one or two people. Their listed qualities included trustworthiness, generosity, being there, readiness to go the extra mile, big-heartedness and being non-judgmental, inspiring and an excellent listener.

Most great leaders have developed these qualities. When a leader offers *reconnaissance* well, the effect resounds in both time and space. It echoes loud and long. It has an effect not only on the individual but also on all those connected to them. It stays in the memory for a very long time and is a powerful way of creating or restoring goodwill. Such a leader is always on the lookout for colleagues who aren't flourishing, trying to find meaningful ways to express gratitude to them. They are aware that they are in a position to do this because of their role, and that the power of their position allows this *reconnaissance* to have a strong effect.

One of the most effective ways to become better at offering gratitude in the form of *reconnaissance* is to find someone who is good at it and try to learn the qualities and skills they model.

I was very fortunate to learn from such a person when I was very young – my mother's boss, Captain Hinchcliffe. My mother would pick us five children up from our primary school and take us back to her workplace for the rest of the afternoon. She was a secretary at the local boat shed.

A lasting memory was the joy my mother exuded on a Friday afternoon. It wasn't just because it was the end of the week. It was because it was the day that Captain Hinchcliffe – a retired British Navy captain and a thorough gentleman – personally gave all his employees their weekly wages. I witnessed a total shift in my mother's demeanor at this moment. A quiet ritual took place as she stood up and he passed the crisp, brown envelope to her. With trueheartedness, he would use that opportunity to tell her all the things he was appreciative of, that she had done for him that week. My mother would be smiling from ear to ear. Captain Hinchcliffe was a master at offering *reconnaissance*.

In later years, hearing my mother's many glowing accounts of Captain Hinchcliffe's impact on her, it was clear that he was also the captain of 'relation-ship'. It was his capacity to offer *reconnaissance* that enabled him to also have stern conversations with my mother and other employees and clients when it was warranted. There was no way that any bullying would take place under the captain's watch. He also forged new territory with some difficult customers who had been hard to deal with in the past, because he gave them time and cared about them and their happiness. His whole demeanor was one of listening attentively. Around him, everyone felt they mattered and that he had time for them. He was able to offer *reconnaissance* to all without favouritism.

When we come across stories like this in our lives, we are more able to set a standard of how to be in relationship with others.

## Cultivating patience

Hopefully the insights you have gained so far have helped you understand why you have resentment and, in turn, have helped you to start to untangle some of the difficult relationships in your life. However, at times you might also feel that you still have a long way to go. You might aim to offer a particular person more *reconnaissance*, for example, but find that just being able to greet them in the mornings is challenging. Progressing to the next step of connecting with them in conversation could feel like a step too far, and you may feel that on the whole, progress is slow and laborious.

However, as the great novelist Paulo Coelho wrote, 'The two hardest tests on the... road are the patience to wait for the right moment and the courage to not be disappointed with what we encounter.'[8] In other words, it's important not to judge ourselves about how fast we are moving, or what results we are seeing.

It's also helpful at these times to check on our 'why' for turning to gratitude, as discussed in Chapter 1. You may be wanting to move towards gratitude because it helps you to feel more connected to others, to remember the good, to help you feel calm or to improve your wellbeing. As discussed in Chapter 2, you might now feel more motivated to practise gratitude so that you can more clearly identify your resentment in order for it to have less of a hold on you. From reading Chapter 3, you might be motivated to practise gratitude to grow your compassion and empathy, so you are able to deal with broken expectations. And in reading this chapter, your 'why' could be so that you are better able to deal with a sense of inferiority by opening yourself up to *reconnaissance* or by giving it to others.

As discussed, resentment can make us feel powerless and unable to make the choice to be grateful, even if we have a strong motivation to do so. This is another reason why we need to be patient with ourselves if we feel we are not making much progress in our difficult relationships. As we will discover in the next chapter, we can strengthen our gratitude practice by choosing an 'inner attitude' of gratitude.

# Chapter 5

## Choosing an inner attitude of gratitude

*Whenever you're in conflict with someone, there is one factor that can make the difference between damaging your relationship and deepening it. That factor is attitude.*

– William James

## The deliciousness of choice

While resentment can trap us in a circle of powerlessness, gratitude reminds us that we can choose a different perspective, a different way of being. Very often though, this can only be achieved when we become more fully conscious of the perspective we are currently operating from. Now that we have spent some time identifying the resentment that we carry and its underlying causes, and reflecting on the impact it has on us and those around us, we can move on to look at the choice that gratitude offers us. When viewing relationships through a 'gratitude or resentment' lens, we have a greater capacity to see how the choice we make helps a relationship to flourish or deteriorate.

However, having unpacked the dynamics of resentment, which include a tendency to blame others for our emotional state, we have seen that resentment often stops us from realising that we have any choice at all. We can be angry and frustrated about how disempowered we feel. We are resentful about the original cause of our pain, as well as how the resentment makes us feel and the damage it's causing us.

This is especially the case with longstanding situations that cause resentment, such as sibling rivalry or a difficult dynamic with a former partner. As already looked at with Gwen in Chapter 2, to admit that we have a choice in how we are responding to the pain that we feel someone else has caused not only makes it seem as if we are letting the person off the hook, but it can also feel as if it's dismissing the extent of our suffering.

When we feel that we have no choice, we can draw great wisdom from the example given to us by Victor Frankl, Austrian psychiatrist and survivor of a World War II Nazi concentration camp where he lost his wife, parents and brother. In his book *Man's Search for Meaning*, Victor Frankl describes in detail his horrific experience of the camp. He explores the difference between those whose spirit was destroyed by their suffering and those who took 'the last of the human freedoms – to choose one's attitude in any given set of circumstances, to choose one's own way'.[1]

In his statement 'to choose one's attitude', Frankl was invoking a universal truth, displayed in the midst of the worst horrors one can imagine, that an essential part of being human is the ability to choose how we respond to life's events. In applying this wisdom to the choice between resentment and gratitude, we can examine how we responded in the past and then embrace our freedom to choose otherwise. Again, out of all the states that rob us of the ability to see that such a choice is possible, resentment is at the top of the list.

However, the idea that we can choose how we react to painful situations, whatever their nature or cause, can be very challenging, especially when we're in the grips of it. Surely, a woman who's suffering from domestic violence can't simply choose to react with gratitude, can she? Could a person suffering an incurable illness be expected to choose gratitude? There are some life events that seem to rob us of this choice. As I have said, I totally agree that in some situations such a choice would feel pretty well impossible.

Rather than interpreting this as a flaw in the argument that we can choose our reaction, I like to think of these situations as inspiration for making the choice when we *can* make it. That's when we can reflect that if we are lucky enough to be in a situation where we feel able to choose how to react, we should take the opportunity to do so. At least this is something we can do.

## Uncovering choices

Not so long ago, I had a rude reminder about the difficulty of doing what I am suggesting here, while going through months of excruciating pain in my head. As mentioned earlier, this was due to a severe bout of shingles, a viral infection that attacks the nervous system. For much of my life, I have been blessed with good health and great energy levels. To be struck by such a debilitating illness came as a shock.

Strong painkillers only provided temporary relief. As weeks of suffering and sleepless nights turned into months, my body weakened. My immune system was kaput. I had so little energy that even the smallest tasks felt impossible. I had no choice but to cancel speaking engagements, turn down keynote invitations, pass my PhD students onto others and pull out of work that I loved. The shooting pain in my head was at its worst when I sat at my computer. Any kind of electronic device became a no-go zone. With nothing to distract me and nowhere to escape to, I just had to sit with my pain.

All of my many years of practising gratitude seemed to go out the window. Although I considered myself well-versed in the role of gratitude in adversity and had taught on this specific topic many times, when it came to finding gratitude in my own experience of intense suffering, quite simply, nothing worked.

My inability to find gratitude when afflicted by shingles showed me that gratitude requires a strength of mind that is severely diminished when we're in strong or chronic physical or mental pain. This was a humbling lesson for me, having always believed in the power of mind over matter. It was time to embark on a new journey to find out how I could access gratitude while I was so weak and in so much pain. What could this experience teach me?

I learned that while most of us can easily choose gratitude in certain kinds of situations, this doesn't apply to all of life's experiences, nor is there such a thing as 'mastering gratitude'. For me, gratitude is not innate. It's something we need to be constantly vigilant about and cultivate mindfully. Most importantly, it is a practice, not a destination. From my experience, just when I feel that I have mastered an aspect of gratitude, something comes along to show me that I have a long way to go. We can always deepen our gratitude.

Even if we are able to find a way to rise above physical pain, it's hard to maintain our gratitude when we are experiencing resentment.

When I reflect on some experiences of betrayal in my life – as well as the pain of rejection I used to feel from my mother – the emotional pain was more excruciating and damaging to my sense of self than the pain of shingles. It also lingered for longer.

My healing journey with shingles also took me to another deep realisation when I visited a naturopath five months after my diagnosis. I travelled quite a distance to see him, as he had been highly recommended. After spending a good hour going through the physical symptoms and possible treatments, he told me that none of them would be very effective if I didn't address the underlying cause. I was shocked when he went on to tell me that in his 20 years of treating patients with shingles, he had found one common characteristic: his clients saw themselves as a victim in some area of their life, and as a result felt a lot of resentment towards a particular person or situation. Unbeknownst to him, here I was, trying to write a book about resentment!

The naturopath then gave me suggestions for what to do next. He invited me to reflect on the situation where I had chosen resentment (and yes, he used the word 'chosen') and resolve to work on it. His homework for me was to see where I was choosing resentment rather than gratitude.

I decided to spend the next few days in quiet reflection. It slowly occurred to me that my resentment came from feelings of bitterness I had held for many years towards my husband because of something that happened early in our marriage. I had told myself that I had forgiven him and had moved on, but I now realised that forgiveness wasn't enough. My husband is a wonderful man, and I am deeply grateful to him for so many things in our lives together, but I was now able to see that sometimes this gratitude was forced or superficial.

I reflected that it hadn't taken much for me to forget my gratitude towards my husband whenever my resentment towards him was triggered in some way.

In uncovering this resentment, I became more aware of this being a choice I was making and that I could choose gratitude instead. Over the next few days, I wrote down gratitude practices that centred around my husband, then looked at finding ways I could incorporate them into my life to validate this choice. At this time, my shingles experience mysteriously turned a corner. I had more vitality than I'd had in months. The 'prescription' from the naturopath wasn't just the reminder to practise gratitude, it was a reminder that I could choose my reaction to this situation.

## Choosing our inner attitude

With all of this in mind, how can we go deeper than our thoughts and emotions in order to make the choice of gratitude a part of our being? As we explored in Chapter 2, resentment causes us to ruminate. No matter how much we will ourselves to be grateful, resentment nearly always wins out as the emotion that seeks justice. The shock of what another has done lodges the resentment in our minds. We therefore need to look to a deeper part of ourselves, where the choice to respond with gratitude is more accessible and effective.

Victor Frankl's gift offers us an insight into the domain of self where gratitude can reside, no matter what is happening in our environment. He identified this as our 'attitude'. I would like to propose that it be referred to as our 'inner attitude': who we are in the depth of our being or character, and the general outlook or perspective through which we orientate ourselves in the world. By focusing here, we are able to stand above, or apart from, our ruminating thoughts and feelings and adopt a big-picture perspective. Whether we are conscious of it or not, our inner attitude sits behind and greatly influences our thoughts, emotions, actions and physical health.[2]

Gratitude and resentment permeate our relationships to such a large extent that by pinpointing these two states, we are able to reveal a powerful dimension of our choice-making. Simply by looking into whether our inner attitude is one of resentment or gratitude, we grow our sense of agency and expand our capacity to step above a given situation and actively choose how we will respond.

In fact, as soon as we start contemplating gratitude more deeply and authentically, we are automatically called on to reflect upon the choice we are making at the depth of our being, our inner attitude. As Margaret Visser says: 'The word *gratitude* stands for the process – freely undertaken and therefore hard to pin down with definitions and generalised explanations – by which a person's attitude changes.'[3] You might have experienced this yourself, where you read or hear the word 'gratitude' and it immediately stirs something in you, a powerful reminder that you can choose how you are responding. It bears repeating that gratitude awakens us to the power of choice. This is one of its most important roles in helping us to address our resentment.

## Sibling rivalry

But surely it can't be just as simple as choosing an inner attitude of gratitude? This was Shelley's question at our book club for school principals, where we were discussing my book *Gratitude in Education: A Radical View*. The group had already known each other very well before starting the book club, and had formed an even closer bond through meeting regularly and sharing where gratitude was difficult in their lives. Shelley declared that she felt it was impossible to contemplate gratitude in relationships where there was long-term resentment. She talked about the dread she felt around the forthcoming wedding of her brother, Jack, with whom she had always had a 'love–hate relationship'. She adored Jack and was very proud of his immense success in the world, but family gatherings were a painful trigger for her.

Shelley was the first-born and her brother came two years later. Not only did she have to contend with the common plight of all the attention going to her younger sibling, she suffered from the favouritism extended to Jack her whole life. Shelley's parents and younger brother were calm, confident and 'very normal'. Shelley was the complete opposite. She was often berated and punished by her parents and teachers for being a 'wild child' who rebelled against rules and found it hard to settle at any task for long. Although she was creative and had many hidden talents, Shelley struggled to fit in and do well at school. To make matters worse, on some occasions her teachers told her that they couldn't believe that she and her 'brilliant and well-behaved' brother came from the same family. She is now a successful and popular school principal, but getting to this point had been a hard journey.

Others in the book club commiserated with her and admitted to having complex relationships with their siblings. If we reflect on the major causes of everyday resentment, it's clear that sibling rivalry is right up there as a situation in which resentment can develop and remain. It's natural for children to believe that they and their siblings should be treated equally by their parents, and they can become resentful when these expectations are not met. In turn, the favouritism showered upon the other sibling automatically makes the less-favoured one feel inferior. There are many resources available now to assist parents to be conscious of this when bringing a new child into the family. Even so, it can be difficult to get right. Birth order can have a huge influence on our perception of fairness regarding how we were treated.

Of course, this is an age-old and well-known problem across the world and across the ages. Stories of resentment arising from sibling rivalry are narrated in the Bible (think Cain and Abel), mythology, fables, literature, plays, films and TV shows. One study found that more than a third of adults between 18 and 65 had hostile or apathetic relationships with their siblings.[4] So, if you are feeling that it's impossible to even contemplate gratitude because you have so much 'justified' resentment towards your parents or sibling/s, you are certainly not alone!

Again, I want to emphasise that I am not coming to this discussion as a therapist and acknowledge upfront that professional help may be needed in starting to untangle this particular part of our ball of string. What I'm offering in this chapter is an exploration of the role gratitude can play in helping us to see that we do have – a choice in how we can respond to painful situations.

Shelley was seeking guidance from our book club group in how she could approach her situation with gratitude. She really struggled with the idea that she could choose a different response, as she had a lifetime of feeling small and insignificant whenever she was at any event with her brother.

## A state of preparedness

I steered our discussion towards the success stories we had heard in previous book club sessions of how the principals, including herself, had practised an approach which I call 'a state of preparedness'.[5] In this practice we focus on preparing our inner attitude, orientating ourselves towards gratitude *before* the day begins, or before we go to an event, or before we are about to interact with someone. We can do this in the shower, in the garden or on the way to work, for example.

We set the tone or atmosphere of gratitude – both inside and outside ourselves – for what is about to take place. We might not be able to be grateful for adversity itself, but by consciously focusing on all the things we *can* be grateful for and filling our being with an awareness of these things, we can develop an inner attitude of gratitude and apply this to the challenging situation we are about to encounter. In other words, a state of preparedness allows us to attend to the kind of *being*, or inner attitude, we are bringing to the *doing*, and this gives us more freedom to choose how we want to react.

Shelley then remembered how she had applied a state of preparedness in a recent appointment at a very difficult school, where there was deep resentment among the staff and school community. After opening her eyes, she started each day by being grateful for what she could see. She then filled herself with gratitude for her young children, the love and support she received from her husband, the beautiful roses in her garden, and the natural beauty she saw on her way to work. She soon started to recover her inner attitude of gratitude and brought this with her as she arrived at the school each morning.

Although Shelley wasn't able to change the situation at the school where she was placed, she was able to change her reaction to it by focusing on her inner attitude and cultivating a grateful state of preparedness. When she chose to approach her situation at the school with gratitude, she was able to problem-solve more easily because she could think clearly. She found that she had better interactions with others and felt calmer and not so stressed. She was able to perform her role more effectively by bringing greater integrity to the conversations she had with others and about others, and was more energised throughout her day.

But despite having had such a great experience with this practice, Shelley had never thought of applying a state of preparedness to the situation with her brother Jack. It only seemed relevant to her professional role, not her personal relationships. She agreed with our group that this would be a perfect opportunity to apply a state of preparedness again.

## Choosing how we want to be in difficult relationships

One of the greatest benefits of a state of preparedness is that we create the conditions for our interactions, allowing us to approach them with a greater awareness and vigilance, thereby avoiding resentment. In terms of difficult relationships, it also allows us to approach forthcoming interactions with a strong point on our compass that helps us to navigate our way. We are consciously 'amplifying the good', as we explored in Chapter 1.

However, we need to be able to acknowledge our resentment. We need to identify it at the level of our inner attitude so that we can clearly establish the choice we are making. Before it came up in the book club, Shelley hadn't really given her feelings towards her brother a name. She felt more empowered to do something about it now that she was able to identify it as resentment. She saw that her resentment was caused by broken expectations and feeling inferior, which assisted her to understand how this dynamic had played out at previous family gatherings: her tight stomach and clenched jaw as she saw her parents' adoring looks towards her brother; her sleepless nights leading up to the event; her disingenuous smile in many family photos as she tried to suppress her pain.

For two weeks before the wedding, Shelley practised a state of preparedness by spending time on her evening walks preparing her inner attitude. Because it was difficult for her to think about what she was grateful for about the forthcoming event, Shelley initially focused on the benefits her experience of sibling rivalry had brought in her role as a principal. It had developed her empathy for others in that situation, for instance, and helped her to be more resilient.

After a few days of reflecting and allowing gratitude to arise for the lessons learned, Shelley was then able to reflect on memories of the good times with her brother and parents and acknowledge what she had received from them. She also practised a state of preparedness towards her brother's future wife, whom for some reason she had never liked. Shelley was able to recognise more of Jack's fiancée's good points and feel grateful that she made Jack so happy.

When she came back to our next book club a few weeks after the wedding, Shelley couldn't wait to tell the group how grateful she was for their input. The day had gone better than she could have ever imagined. Rather than dreading it and feeling anxious about what she thought was going to happen, Shelley told us that her inner attitude of gratitude helped her to feel calm and centred. At the wedding, although there were some tense moments, on the whole her communication with everyone was remarkably harmonious. She even showed us a family photo in which she looked genuinely happy.

Because this was such a challenging situation, Shelley said that she had really appreciated the support of the book club to help her become strong and accountable, and to have a firm commitment to her new choice, in readiness for the wedding. From my experience, whenever we truly want to bring such consciousness to our lives, there will be people around us who are willing to assist or who model it in their own lives. Indeed, it's wise to avail ourselves of their wisdom and assistance and seek it out when we need it.

## For things to change first I must change

Shelley came to the understanding that she had a clear choice: to be victim to her anxiety around the wedding and the resentment of ongoing sibling rivalry, or to choose otherwise. For her, the lightbulb moment came when she recognised that she *could* choose. She was able to centre herself and witness what was going on more objectively. There was something else that Shelley experienced. She excitedly told us that everyone in her family was unusually warm and inclusive of her, both in the lead-up to the wedding and on the day itself. In many of our discussions, the book club members have mentioned that their choice of inner attitude seemed to have a direct impact on others around them. They relayed many experiences of tricky situations with certain staff members, for example, and noticed that just by changing their inner attitude, the communication became smoother. When we are ahead of the game and prepare our being with gratitude, others seem to feel this even before we interact with them. Whether we are conscious of it or not, the vibrations of our inner attitude influence those around us.

However, as discussed, we can't control others or how they think, and nor should we even try. We can choose to change, but it should never be done with the expectation that it will lead to others changing. Sometimes it does, and sometimes it doesn't. It's really up to them.

The participants of the book club were school principals, so their inner attitude had the power to set the tone for their whole school. They could 'lead with gratitude' by taking note of areas where they would like to see positive changes and see this as a reflection of something they might need to change in their own inner attitude. When we make these appropriate changes ourselves, often others will follow, even if this doesn't happen straight away or in the way we envisage. However, when we lead with gratitude in our inner attitude, others around us often become more grateful.[6, 7, 8]

If you have a leadership position – and that can include being a parent, a CEO, a soccer coach, a store manager or a teacher – knowing that your inner attitude could well be influencing the inner attitude of those you are leading can form a strong 'why' for moving from resentment towards gratitude.

To develop more capacity to lead with gratitude, our goal could be to imagine our day ahead and think of someone we feel resentful towards, or a person who we know feels resentful towards us. We can imagine ourselves approaching the situation with an inner attitude of gratitude and reflect on what we can be grateful for in that person – what we have received from them.

## Gratitude for past choices

So far, we have explored how we can practise a state of preparedness for challenging encounters in the present and in the future, but when we start to feel empowered to make different choices, we sometimes feel guilt or shame about holding on to resentment for so long.

Although we aren't able to change the choices we made in the past, we can change our reaction to these choices. Gratitude has an important role to play here. We can look back on past pain and be grateful for what we have learned from it; we can approach it with an inner attitude of gratitude and be more forgiving of ourselves. As Shelley recognised, there were things to be grateful for in the situation with Jack. It eventually led her to becoming a successful principal with a strong reputation for fighting for equity for her staff and students.

One of the paradoxes of resentment is that while we need to do everything possible to free ourselves of it, we can also be grateful for what it has taught us. This is an important dynamic of gratitude and resentment – where we can be grateful for resentment itself. In fact, very often it's only gratitude for what the resentment has taught us that can do this vital healing of our past, allowing us to even contemplate gratitude towards the person we feel has wronged us.

It's only when we accept that resentment is part of our everyday interactions, part of the human condition, that we can acknowledge its role in allowing us to discover more about ourselves and our relationships with others. As philosopher Amélie Rorty argues, the importance of resentment 'lies in serving as an indication – a symptom – of things that have gone wrong, things that require acknowledgment and remedy'.[9]

Our insights into resentment show us that something is amiss, that our personal boundaries have been stepped over or that our expectations have not been met in some way. Resentment helps us to be more self-defining.

When we recognise resentment, we simultaneously receive an invitation to work on ourselves and our difficult relationships. Without this we may not expand ourselves and grow our character. We might be able to see that resentment gave us greater resilience and grew our empathy for those who have been through similar situations. Through recognising our own resentment, we are able to become more aware of its signs in others, and this can help us to be more competent in addressing conflict. When we are able to identify our resentment and its underlying causes, we are able to gain deeper insight into ourselves and others.

\*\*\*

So far in this book, we have explored the notion of deep gratitude, which is highly relational and involves acting on what we are grateful for through expressing our gratitude in heartfelt and purposeful ways. We have also discovered that we need to express gratitude in ways that are authentic to us and meaningful to the other person. Focusing on the inner attitude with which we are approaching our practice of gratitude is important to this reflection process.

In all the stories shared so far, we can see the dimension of inner attitude at play. We can see how our inner attitude influences our actions and how our actions can deepen our inner attitude of gratitude. I've summarised this in the following diagram.

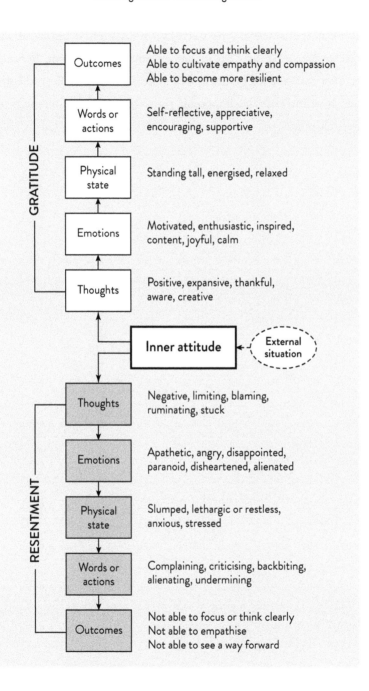

In the next chapter, you will discover that all you have learned about resentment so far can help you understand self-resentment. In order to offer true-hearted gratitude to another in ways that are authentic and have integrity, it's important to move from *self*-resentment to *self*-gratitude.

# Chapter 6

## From self-resentment to self-gratitude

*The perfect is the enemy of the good.*

*– Voltaire*

### Falling short of our own expectations

Most of Andrew's colleagues and students spoke glowingly about him as a brilliant teacher. Within five years after he graduated, he had won an award for innovative practice and contribution to the profession. However, the view that others had of him was completely different from how Andrew felt inside. No matter how much praise he received, he had a core belief that he wasn't worthy. He often put in all-nighters during the week and worked over the whole weekend, trying to design the perfect lesson plan or write the most eloquent and detailed student reports. Yet he never felt that anything he did was good enough.

Andrew often felt stressed and anxious. His nights were often filled with mental torture, when he thought over and over about what he'd said or didn't say to a particular student or colleague and wished that he had reacted otherwise. He went through the day's lessons again and again in his mind and thought about various students' responses, berating himself for mistakes he felt he had made.

Andrew's path to teaching had been a very rocky one. He had dropped out of school early and had always regretted this, as he felt he had let himself and his family down. He believed he was inferior to his peers because he saw himself as less educated. He felt that dropping out had robbed him of opportunities and resulted in him being unable to attract the kind of girlfriends some of his friends had.

Andrew became obsessed with trying to gain back his personal power, to overcome his broken expectations of himself and regain what he believed was his true capacity. With enormous struggle, he returned to school and made it through to the end, but this process added further humiliation because he was, by then, an adult. Once he got to university, things seemed to settle for a while, but he suffered from 'imposter syndrome', never quite believing in his abilities and feeling that he shouldn't be there, anxious that someone would discover that he was a fraud. Andrew's obsession with proving himself a capable student led him to have unrealistic expectations of himself. He overworked his assignments and chronically procrastinated.

Andrew's choice to take up teaching was driven by a burning desire to make a difference to students like him. He wanted to be a teacher who could recognise those who weren't flourishing and encourage them to continue in their education, no matter what. However, he still had the pattern of over-striving and feeling like he never measured up to his own or others' expectations of him. No matter how hard he tried, he couldn't shake off the shame he felt about his decision to drop out of school early.

When he became a teacher, he continued all these patterns. Although he sometimes felt competent and content in his role, there were also occasions when he would feel paranoid, thinking that others could see that he really wasn't as good as people were saying. He would latch onto any evidence that, in his mind, confirmed that he was a failure, and ignore the data that said he was an excellent teacher.

Andrew had mastered a number of ways to make himself feel inferior.

## Identifying self-resentment

As we have discussed, resentment can often be hidden. Self-resentment is often even harder to find. In many cases, self-resentment has its source in childhood or adolescence, and it can take a long time to discover that there is another way to be.

Self-resentment can play out in a variety of ways. It makes us take things personally. It diminishes our self-regard, self-esteem and self-confidence. It can even become a part of our persona, whereby we tend to put ourselves down and admire others and their achievements more than we do our own. Self-resentment arises from the disappointment and inferiority we feel when we fail to meet our own expectations, and from comparing ourselves to others.

We have previously explored how resentment attracts more resentment. In the same way, self-resentment grows as it attracts confirmation of a strongly held belief around not being good enough or making a mess of things. We become our own worst enemy by confirming this belief in a variety of self-defeating ways.

Andrew's story of self-resentment is echoed to some degree by many of the pre-service teachers who come to my classes. They have a chronic tendency to give themselves a hard time. They suffer so much stress and anxiety if they don't get everything right the first time. Indeed, I have seen them walk out of some of my tutorials looking traumatised because they think others have done a better job than them at presenting a mock lesson. When doing their practice teaching in schools, they mistakenly believe that they have to demonstrate the same mastery as their supervising teacher. They tend to beat themselves up if they are unable to do this.

On the surface it can seem that this strong reaction is coming from envy or competitiveness. However, delving a little more deeply shows that it often comes from measuring themselves against their expectations and feeling that they never make the grade.

Of course, this isn't only present in people who are starting out in a new profession. Self-resentment arising from broken expectations was also a common theme in my book clubs with principals, as well as in my workshops with elite athletes and coaches. In the latter case, the person they were most disappointed with if they didn't win gold or do well in a competition was themselves. Self-resentment kept them awake at night as they replayed events, berating themselves for the choices they made with negative self-talk. If only they had trained harder, not missed that session, had earlier nights, taken the corner in a more skilful way during the race. This continued for years and wreaked havoc in their lives, robbing them of joy and contentment, while at the same time setting up a cycle of self-resentment.

We can, in a very real sense, be making ourselves sick with our own disappointment in ourselves – disappointment that can't be addressed if we don't recognise and acknowledge it.

## Self-resentment and regret

Another way of identifying self-resentment is to distinguish it from regret. Although very painful, some would say that regret is a positive thing. If we can reflect on some of the poor decisions we have made, we can learn from our mistakes and be motivated to do better in the future. There's a sense of moving forward with the wisdom of hindsight. We feel we can change for the better. Andrew was full of regret for having left school early. However, this morphed into self-resentment because he wasn't able to let go of his disappointment in himself and release the stuck feelings.

Where regret offers wisdom, self-resentment causes us to berate ourselves to the point where we can't even see the lesson. We can't let go, and we feel that we have no choice but to suffer the consequences and have them define us and our life story forever. For Andrew, his self-resentment had started to influence his whole identity.

The element of choice and responsibility is important in making the distinction between regret and self-resentment. With regret, we feel we can take responsibility for the choices we made. In the case of self-resentment, there appears to be no other choice but to drown in the disappointment we feel towards ourselves.

Here, gratitude plays an important role in enabling us to make better choices at the point of regret, so that it doesn't develop into self-resentment. When we realise that we have made a mistake, if we are able to be grateful for the lesson learned, this will amplify its many benefits and help us to move on. We could be grateful for what the lesson is teaching us about how to grow and change so that we can become a better person, or someone who is more resilient. We can also be grateful for our self-acceptance rather than allowing self-resentment to take over.

## The perfection of imperfection

Andrew had reached a critical point in his teaching. He was feeling burnt out and his health was deteriorating. He was stressed and anxious and was losing his original desire to make a difference to his students. His enthusiasm and motivation were sharply declining, and he was starting to do what felt to him to be a half-hearted job on his lessons and reports. Andrew's growing indifference to his teaching and his students increased his sense of failure and self-resentment. He felt worse about himself and started to take days off in which he just zoned out in front of the TV for hours. He was becoming unrecognisable to himself, as well as to his students and colleagues.

Andrew's experience is a classic example of what happens when we can't reach our ideal of perfection. We give up. We aim for perfection or nothing, and there is nothing in between. Striving for perfection often also leads to procrastination. We're terrified that what we produce won't be good enough, so we don't try. As Voltaire warns, 'The perfect is the enemy of the good.'

Perfectionism is often a primary cause of self-resentment. As 'perfect' is out of reach and completely unrealistic, it means that we are never satisfied and are constantly disappointed in ourselves. We compare ourselves with others who seem better than us, and we never feel that who we are or what we do is good enough. At worst, we blame others for the situation, as it's too painful to look at our own mistakes. To acknowledge our shortcomings can be much too difficult if we are only satisfied with perfection.

An important gratitude practice in addressing self-resentment is to explore our notion of what perfection is. In many ways the idea of something being perfect is, in itself, essentially flawed. By its nature, perfection can never be achieved, because if we look deeply there is always something that can be improved. As we saw with Andrew, striving for perfection is always accompanied by a degree of uncertainty or anxiety. It locks us into the belief that there is a clearly defined example of perfection that looks a certain way, and all we need to do is achieve it. Once we have reached it, there will be nothing else to strive for and therefore nothing more to learn.

We can find a happy balance by trying our best but at the same time recognising the imperfection of perfection, and even being grateful for this. The ancient Japanese philosophy of *wabi-sabi* encompasses this beautifully. In tea ceremonies, the bowls that are most highly valued were those that had an uneven glaze or cracks, or were shaped irregularly. These imperfections contributed to the beauty of the object. This tradition speaks of taking pleasure in the imperfect, a celebration of the way things are rather than the way they should be. Instead of hiding faults or being ashamed of them, they can be brought out into the open and celebrated.

## A healthy balance

Although in the end Andrew decided to stay in the profession, talented young teachers like him are leaving in droves because they feel burnt out, unsupported, undervalued and disillusioned. I believe that one of the underlying causes is that they don't know how to manage their perfectionism and the accompanying self-resentment. They may not be able to take in the gratitude that others are giving them – and therefore gain from the accompanying resilience and sense of self-value – because they are always on the lookout for their mistakes and failings.

Another contemporary source of self-resentment stems from the expectations we set up around having a perfect work–life balance. We might find that we overcommit to being a perfect partner, parent, friend or sibling, or having a perfect body. At the same time, we're keeping all the balls in the air so that we can be perfect in our work as well. If we're not meeting our expectations in any of these areas – which is certain to be the case – we can become self-resentful in every one of them. This could involve a state of constant disappointment and broken expectations about how we are 'failing' to measure up to the self-defined perfect self. In turn, these resentments feed upon each other, as they did with the powerful self-resentment Andrew felt about his perceived incapacity to study or teach well.

Sadly, this striving for perfection can also do immense damage to our self-worth. Self-resentment leads to self-loathing. We are plagued by a sense that we have failed to meet our own – and society's – expectations of what we should look like and how we should behave. We feel inferior in the presence of others who we feel look better, or who are doing better than us. We set ourselves up with a range of regimes to achieve 'perfection', which only fuels our self-resentment when we let ourselves down by not being able to stick to them.

Some people may think that the way forward is to have no expectations of ourselves, or to lower our expectations so that we don't give ourselves such a hard time by failing to meet them. However, as discussed in Chapter 3, lowering our expectations is not a wise way out of resentment because it means settling for mediocrity or lowering our standards for who we want to be. It might make us even more disappointed in ourselves.

If Andrew had had no expectations of himself as a teacher, he wouldn't have suffered so much, but he also wouldn't have become the great teacher he often was. He almost certainly wouldn't have won that prestigious teaching award.

A more positive way forward is to have high expectations but to develop the self-awareness not to be disappointed or resent ourselves if we don't meet them. Accepting less than perfection doesn't mean giving up our expectations of doing our best. It means having more realistic expectations of what 'best' means and having healthier ways of welcoming 'imperfection'. We can also apply the wisdom of *wabi-sabi*, where we even celebrate our imperfections.

When we find ourselves laughing at our mistakes, discussing them openly with others without any stress or anxiety and sharing the lessons we have learned along the way, we know we are starting to untangle the difficult relationship we are having with ourselves.

## Moving towards self-gratitude

We can draw on what we have explored so far about the nature of gratitude and see how it applies to self-gratitude. This is an important step. As already mentioned, many are far better at expressing gratitude to others than to themselves. When you have self-gratitude, you have empathy and compassion for yourself and are nourished by opening yourself up to what you receive from others, not just what you give them. You have great appreciation for your inherent worth as a human being, and spend time acknowledging your good points and being grateful for them as a way of amplifying the good you feel about yourself. Self-gratitude teaches us to celebrate the perfection of our imperfections because we are grateful for our perceived failures or shortcomings. Such gratitude can increase our self-acceptance and enable us to do something positive about addressing our mistakes – if we choose to do so.

Instead of looking at the graph that has 100 per cent as the one and only target, and therefore feeling self-resentment about what we haven't done, we can orientate ourselves to the 0 per cent starting point on the graph and express gratitude for what we have been able to achieve. We can stop striving for perfection and instead celebrate the small gains, noticing and building on them.

In this process, it is important to watch the self-talk we use, and in particular the labels we give ourselves. For instance, instead of using the label 'perfectionist', it would be more helpful to see ourselves as having a *perfection perspective*. If we call ourselves a perfectionist, it implies that this is part of who we are – like some kind of personality disorder that we can't change. However, I have seen many who have been able to shift their perspective and orientate themselves to a much gentler and more accepting relationship with themselves, once they acquire the self-awareness and skills to do so and accept the perfection of imperfection.

There are many other gratitude practices that help to increase self-gratitude. One of the most powerful of these is a gratitude journal. There are all kinds of versions of this process. This is most effective for me: before going to sleep, I write down everything I am grateful for on that day, and an area of my character I would like to change or a way I can give back to another out of acknowledgment of my gratitude. Simply taking note of what we receive from others and the world at large enables us to be more open to what life gives us.

To grow our self-gratitude, it's important to take note of our good points, even if this is just gratitude for getting through days that are tough. We can also include what we have given to others and how we might give back to ourselves through celebrating or nurturing ourselves in some way.

If we have strong self-resentment, it can be difficult to immediately recognise what we are grateful for about ourselves. Andrew had heard about the strategy of using a gratitude journal from one of his colleagues and decided to give it a go. For the first few weeks, it was hard for him to stop beating himself up for not being more grateful in the past. He also initially wondered if he was doing the journal well enough or practising gratitude as 'perfectly' as he possibly could. By recognising that gratitude is a practice which we develop over time, rather than something we get right or feel comfortable with immediately, Andrew began to take note of the small things – the taste of his coffee and the smile of the person who served it to him, sunshine, warmth, delicious food. He also included what he was grateful for about himself: that he had achieved so much in spite of great adversity; that he was liked by his students; that he had good health.

After a few weeks of writing in his journal every day about what he was grateful for in himself, Andrew noticed some of his feelings of inadequacy were diminishing. There were more and more days where he felt not only happy but more than happy with himself. He judged himself less for what he didn't do, or didn't do perfectly, and focused more on what he did do, and did well. This even meant that he stopped giving himself a hard time if he occasionally forgot to write in his journal or was too tired to do so, and was grateful to himself for his shift in perspective.

## Opening up to another's gratitude

When Andrew was full of self-resentment, he would dismiss any expressions of gratitude from his students or colleagues, thinking, 'You don't know what you're talking about,' or 'I'm not good enough for that.' Their offers of *reconnaissance*, no matter how meaningful or sincere, only made Andrew feel worse. He felt undeserving. He also sometimes doubted the truth of their statements and thought that they were just trying to be nice or flatter him for their own purposes. Unfortunately, people who feel that their gratitude is rejected are less likely to offer gratitude again. This was indeed what Andrew found as he was less and less appreciated by his peers.

However, Andrew's newfound gratitude for himself opened the doorway to recognising when others expressed gratitude to him. He was able to stop and savour such moments, and return to them in his gratitude journal. He no longer rejected the acts of *reconnaissance* he was receiving from others, and instead learned how to genuinely offer gratitude for them. This was another cause for celebration.

It was around this time that Andrew received a gratitude letter from a student, Jared, whom he had taught in his first year of teaching. He had received other such letters in the past, but his self-resentment hadn't allowed him to take in the words and he had quickly put them aside. Now that he was practising self-gratitude, he was really able to savour Jared's kind words.

Jared thanked Andrew for all that he had done for him, sharing his memories of some of Andrew's great lessons. He thanked Andrew for noticing his abilities and potential when other teachers and those around him appeared to have lost hope for him. He said that he would never have been able to finish his apprenticeship and land his dream job without Andrew's care and wonderful teaching.

The *reconnaissance* – recognition through gratitude – Jared offered Andrew at this time, and Andrew's newfound ability to take it in, grew his self-gratitude exponentially. It was a real turning point in being able to move from self-resentment to self-gratitude. When Andrew relayed his story to me, he said that Jared's letter was 'an anchor of hope to my soul'.

Andrew now felt less anxious and was able to appreciate things more fully. He was more able to accept himself with all his flaws and was less judgmental. He felt calmer and happier than he had in years. His growing empathy and compassion for himself was extending to others. He laughed and smiled more about his mistakes. He was more relaxed going to work and found joy in teaching again.

Andrew was also able to be more grateful to his students and recognise things in them that he had never seen before. He was able to recover one of the most crucial aspects of the craft of teaching by approaching his students with gratitude for what he received from them, rather than simply focusing on the mistakes they made.

## Establishing stronger boundaries

Over time, Andrew's newfound self-gratitude showed him that he needed to form a different kind of relationship with many people in his life. In the past, he had put their needs before his own due to his low self-worth. He used to lose himself in their world, until he eventually came to the realisation that others' needs or happiness were not more important than his own. This allowed him to establish clearer boundaries around how he wanted to be treated.

This was also an important lesson learned by Natalie, who challenged me after a recent gratitude workshop. She asked me if there was danger in trying to be grateful in situations where we are being treated badly. Natalie then recounted, with much pain, the situation with her employer and his regular put-downs over the past year. Whenever Natalie tried to talk to him about it, he was dismissive. For a long time, she did her best to try to put up with his belittling behaviours so she could keep her job. Finally, however, she had to leave.

Natalie confessed that the very suggestion of the need to feel grateful made her feel defensive. She questioned the legitimacy of gratitude in the situation with her boss. My reply was that until we can feel self-gratitude, it's almost impossible to make decisions that are honouring our integrity and wellbeing in the midst of conflict with another. Sometimes it's a lack of gratitude to self that gives them power over us in the first place.

When I shared with Natalie my belief that leaving her work situation, painful as it was, was a powerful way of expressing gratitude to herself, she was able to see the relevance of gratitude. Natalie recognised that if she had stayed, she would have continued to be undermined and would have had nothing to draw on to give to others or herself. Natalie was able to see that gratitude isn't about being grateful all the time to all people – or in this case, to her boss. It's about accessing gratitude from where we *can* access it. She felt relieved when she realised this.

If we are grateful to ourselves, our cup of self-love starts to fill, and we are more able to deal with our resentment in proactive rather than reactive ways. Each time we do this, we are 'self-defining' by standing up for who we are and how we want to be treated.

Sometimes, we first need to address our beliefs and feelings of inferiority. Through having strong boundaries and not allowing ourselves to be bullied, insulted or ridiculed by another, we are at the same time expressing self-gratitude. We often hear the statement that before we can love another, we first need to love ourselves. Gratitude helps us recognise more of our own inner beauty, skills, talents and achievements, and how we are able to use these to give to others and the world.

At the same time though, we should be vigilant about never allowing our self-gratitude to morph into self-adoration or a feeling of being superior to others, or using our newfound sense of self to put others down. If this were to happen, self-gratitude would lose its essential characteristics of humility and the awareness of our inherent interconnectedness with others. We need to be ever mindful of the fact that gratitude, by its very nature, involves the relationship between giver, receiver and gift. Self-gratitude is an acknowledgment of everything we give and a humble recognition that we are who we are today because of everything we have received.

Natalie was able to recognise that since leaving her workplace, her gratitude to self had grown exponentially because she felt a greater sense of self-worth. Andrew was able to find a new group of friends, and this in itself helped him to continue to establish stronger boundaries around how he wanted to treat himself and be treated – with gratitude.

## Self-discovery

Andrew used to shy away from taking time to reflect on himself for fear of seeing something less than perfect; however, his newfound self-gratitude helped him to embrace a new way of being – 'discovery' mode. In discovery mode we are consciously and fearlessly looking for imperfections – for data that says we are off course, for where we might be able to do better – and being proactive in readjusting our course. We see mistakes as a place to discover more about ourselves and others. We are humble and accept that we are not perfect, and therefore are less likely to judge ourselves and others. Rather than feeling anxious and stressed, we feel light, energetic and motivated.

As we practise this art of discovery, we consciously orientate ourselves towards what we can be grateful for. Rather than dwelling on the past with remorse and regret, or dreading the future in case we might get it wrong, we're excited about what these can teach us and how they could help us to grow. We treat each day as a new day for which we are grateful – a new day full of possibility and learning.

In this mode, we are on the lookout for self-resentment and are willing to address it with self-gratitude. We focus on what we love about ourselves and all that we give and have been given. Our self-gratitude gives us confidence. We are clear and accepting about our limitations and aim for the best without over-striving. This helps us to move towards joy and balance. We are kinder to ourselves and others.

\*\*\*

In this chapter we have explored how easy it is for self-resentment to take hold, and that this arises from the same causes as the resentment we feel towards another: we resent ourselves when we break our own expectations and when we feel inferior to others. How these causes manifest differently in self-resentment is that they often have their origins in a distorted notion of what it means to be perfect. Gratitude to self is a powerful way of shifting the perception of perfection to that of celebrating our imperfections. Gratitude to self also has us aiming for a healthy balance in our lives, so that we are grateful for what we do have and what we can achieve.

We'll know that we are being more grateful to ourselves if we can take in the gratitude expressed to us from another and really feel it and believe it. We can see it in our thoughts, self-talk, physical state and relationships. We will feel more connected, confident, accepting, abundant and able to appreciate our own capacities and skills more fully. This will result in us relating more strongly to others and the world around us, and allowing that world to mirror our self-worth.

So far, we have explored the role of gratitude in addressing the resentment we feel towards others, and towards ourselves. Now we are going to delve into how gratitude can help us to deal with the resentment that is directed towards us by others, and how the self-gratitude we've discussed in this chapter is a crucial first step.

# Chapter 7

# Addressing another's resentment towards us

*Not everything that is faced can be changed,*
*but nothing can be changed until it is faced.*

– James Baldwin

## Identifying another's resentment

Those of you who have been on the receiving end of another's resentment will know how painful it is, and how hard it is not to respond resentfully in turn. You will also know how difficult it is to untangle the complexities that have led to this impasse. There are usually many layers of misunderstanding or pain, and the deeper you go the harder it gets. Dealing with our own resentment is often easier than dealing with another's resentment towards us.

There are some situations where we feel sure that somebody holds resentment towards us but we can't understand why, and we feel that it is totally unjustified. In other situations, someone might be dumping their resentment on us, but actually the cause is something else that is not related to us at all. The gratitude practices we would employ in this situation will be touched on in the next chapter. In this chapter, we are going to discuss the confronting and awkward realisation that we need to take some responsibility for the role we have played in damaging the relationship, manifesting in the other person's resentment.

When a resentful person feels they are justified in their feelings, and because they are feeling hurt, they often believe that the one who has caused the resentment should make the first move. However, that person may not even know what the problem is.

How we respond to another's resentment can change the relationship forever. One of the most destructive responses is no response at all. In this case, the resentment will fester and the other person will more than likely not want to bring it up with us again. Moreover, if they are in pain and we are not, it can be easy to misunderstand and to judge them as silly for holding a grudge. If our thoughts run along these lines, this only adds fuel to the fire.

Because it all seems too difficult, we might feel that it's just easier if we avoid the person and hope that things will be smoothed over with time. However, you probably already know that this strategy isn't likely to work. Resentment tends to fester if it's not addressed, and the other person's rejection and undermining of us won't necessarily stop. The strategy of ceasing to communicate, casting the resentful person out of our life or friendship group, also doesn't work in the long term either. Even though we may not be physically present in each other's lives, the antagonism and hurt will live on in our hearts. Throughout this book we are exploring a different way forward, where we are putting the repair and restoration of the relationship at the heart of our 'why'. Ultimately, this is the only path to deep and lasting resolution both within ourselves and with the other person.

Each of the gratitude practices explored in this chapter apply to personal relationships, regardless of the context. You will discover from the following story how Simon, a managing director in a large IT business, found his way through a mass of resentment from his staff. Leaders have a particularly powerful and important role to play in such a situation. Their ability to identify and address resentment in a positive way can make or break their organisation and have an enduring impact on staff morale and wellbeing.

## Seeing our blind spots

Over the previous decade in his role as managing director, Simon had been sure that he was running a tight ship; there had been no major discontent under his watch. Most of the staff seemed fairly happy, and clients – his main yardstick of success – reported being satisfied with the company's products. He knew that there was a bit of moaning and backbiting among some employees, but he put that down to the personality differences that are found in every organisation. He sensed that some staff didn't like him, but he accepted that good managers are not necessarily universally liked – a motto he had taken on board rather literally since attending a leadership course. Simon also knew that there was a high turnover of staff in some sections of the organisation, and high rates of sick leave in others, but again he just put this down to lifestyle choices rather than anything that reflected upon his management style.

He wasn't too worried when the CEO asked him to distribute an anonymous survey of satisfaction and confidence ratings among his employees. But when the results came in, Simon was shocked. He received extremely low scores on nearly all indicators related to his style of leadership: confidence, respect, trust and morale. The comments weren't limited to petty grievances and outbursts of annoyance. Many clearly came from feelings of deep-seated resentment. Most staff said that they dreaded coming to work; many said that their workplace made them ill or that they would leave if they could afford to. About a quarter reported that they had been on the receiving end of bullying.

What hurt and shattered Simon the most was that he had expected that at least half of the staff would give glowing reports about his style of leadership. After all, he had recently granted them a pay rise and given them even better working conditions than they'd asked for. He had also expected loyalty from his group of middle managers, who knew precisely the kind of pressures all managing directors were under. He felt betrayed, because it was obvious to him from the words used in some of the answers to the survey that his middle managers were very unhappy. This made Simon wonder if they had been dishonest in all their dealings with him – being nice to his face but trashing him in this faceless survey.

Simon's health deteriorated rapidly. He experienced symptoms of high stress and anxiety, as well as back pain and headaches. His resentment escalated towards the staff and managers, but also to the CEO, who he started to suspect had deliberately orchestrated the survey as a way of undermining him and preparing the way for him to be sacked. His resilience diminished and his integrity began to crumble, causing paranoia, shame and spiralling self-doubt.

Then he received a meeting request from the CEO to look at the results of the survey and discuss the strategies he planned to put in place to redress the situation. He really needed to do something, and fast.

Simon called a special meeting with his eight managers and asked them to explain to him what the survey results meant from their perspective. He hadn't slept much the night before and didn't handle the meeting well. He berated them for not coming directly to tell him about their own and their staff members' dissatisfaction and accused them of hiding things from him. Simon couldn't see his own blind spots and was not able to take responsibility for the outcomes of his behaviour and manner. All he did was blame others for keeping him in the dark and for the results of the survey. He projected his pain and anger onto them.

Most responded by looking away as Simon went into his tirade, but a few piped up and sheepishly said that he was always busy and focused on the products and clients. They said they thought he didn't really care about how the staff were going. Very angry and trying to defend his identity and position, Simon shut them down with more recriminations, refusing to listen to those who were courageous enough to offer the feedback he said he wanted.

When he met with his CEO, his resentment had escalated further, and he gave her a long list of evidence of the incompetence of his middle management team. He even suggested that a few should be fired or made redundant. In the middle of his rant, the CEO asked him to stop. She asked him to talk to her about his role in contributing to these results. She was firm in telling him that she would invest in a personal coach for him for the next few months and at a later date she would meet with him again. Simon was particularly furious when she told him that the coach she had in mind specialised in gratitude strategies!

## Self-reflection

Although he rebelled against the idea of a coach, Simon realised that he really did need some kind of support in order to address his situation. His physical ailments were sending him that message loud and clear, but he procrastinated. He postponed meetings with Michael, his appointed coach, several times at short notice, and when they finally did meet for the first time, Simon quickly got upset and angry.

Simon had hoped that Michael would just give him some simple strategies so that he could sort things out with his managers and at least get them to show him more loyalty. He was shocked when Michael suggested that he start by taking the focus off others completely and stop trying to get them to behave differently. Instead, he was to focus entirely on himself. Not only that, but he was to do this exclusively for the next month at least!

Simon was certain that it wasn't going to take that long for him to change, and he challenged Michael accordingly. He also said that it wouldn't stop the staff complaints from escalating even more. He feared that his CEO would think that he wasn't doing anything to address the problem.

Michael invited Simon to reflect on this principle: *For things to change, first I must change.* In their discussions over the following weeks, it slowly dawned on Simon that this was the only way forward.

Although it was difficult for Simon, they looked at the responses in the survey together and tried to isolate the main areas that indicated what changes Simon needed to make. It was clear that his staff held deep-seated anger and disappointment about the way Simon had made them feel. The heart of most of their responses could be explained in one word: resentment.

Michael asked Simon what, if he could see this situation in a mirror, it would reflect to him about himself. Where did *he* have resentment towards his staff? Simon needed to realise that before he could expect to understand the resentment of the staff, he needed to address his own.

At first, Simon said that he didn't harbour any resentment towards his staff, now or in the past. Yet his fists were clenched, his body was tense and his face was red when he said it. When questioned about the number of sick days he had taken since receiving the survey results, Simon had to confess that his ongoing health issues and insomnia were indications of how betrayed he felt. Reflecting on the weeks that followed the survey results, he was able to see that many of his escalating ailments had resentment at their core.

Through Michael's tactful but deep questioning, Simon was able to identify areas where he had been slandering and undermining others. Recently this had been to alleviate some of the pain, to attempt to share some of the burden and to get empathy from those he had considered to be his friends. He was now able to realise that this only further undermined trust and collegiality. Simon was also able to admit that this wasn't anything new. He had developed a habit of sharing with others his negative thoughts about staff who had disappointed him – especially down at the pub on a Friday night.

Simon admitted to gossiping about his CEO especially. When she had been appointed, Simon had been insulted that he hadn't been considered for the position and, deep down, even questioned her ability to do the job because she was a woman. He started to see that he had dealt with the blow to his ego by slandering her when he had the opportunity. This was the reflection in the mirror that Simon needed to see the most. He didn't realise at the time that when we bring down a leader with mindless slander and backbiting, we bring down the whole organisation. It was no wonder that his staff were resentful.

In order to see how our reflection is mirrored in situations of others' resentment towards us, we have to take the focus off the pain that we feel others have caused us and focus instead on the pain we have caused them. If we don't, then we will inevitably respond to their resentment through the lens of our own resentment – which can only lead to further distortion and conflict.

## Building gratitude

Many hard truths were slowly dawning on Simon about his own part in the organisation's culture of resentment and complaint. But there was also a lot he couldn't see because of his crumbling resilience. He felt so broken down and sickened by the survey results. It was very difficult for him to talk about it anymore. His self-resentment soared sky-high as his blind spots were revealed, and he felt so battered and ashamed that any attempts to address the resentment with his staff were unlikely to succeed.

Michael helped Simon to see that first of all, he needed to build his personal resilience. In order to do so, and to find the humility and courage to go on, he needed to draw on the fortifying powers of gratitude. Again, he resisted. It seemed totally insane to him that he should respond to this situation with gratitude. He thought this meant that Michael would have him walking around the place all bright and smiling. This was until Michael showed him that gratitude starts with a very individual and internal process, and no one else needed to know. He also showed Simon some research on how gratitude can build our resilience when going through hard times.[1]

It became apparent that it was important for Simon to enter into this process of gratitude by taking small steps forward. Although it was difficult for him to find anything he could be grateful for in the situation at work, Michael encouraged Simon to focus on what he could be grateful for *outside* the situation. When prompted, Simon decided to focus on the gratitude he felt for his delightful grandchild, his beautiful garden, his comfortable home and the peaceful neighbourhood where he lived. He grew this awareness by listing five things that he was grateful for at the end of every day.

To help him to cultivate self-gratitude, Michael guided Simon to write down things he could be grateful for about himself – the fact that he had the courage to change and turn up for work even though he knew there was so much antagonism; his many skills in helping clients; his generosity to his children and grandchild.

Despite his original skepticism, Simon was surprised to see that gratitude did make a difference. He became more able to approach his days at work with optimism instead of bitterness. He was actually beginning to cope better. He felt calmer and more able to face going to work in the mornings. He started to sleep better.

This also made it easier for Simon to revisit the survey more objectively and to start to see a way forward, a light at the end of tunnel. Although it was hard, he began to see the staff responses as a cry for change and was now beginning to change from within himself.

## Looking for signs of disquiet

As discussed, it's often much easier to hide away from another's resentment towards us than to address it. We can go into denial, put the blame back on them or respond with our own animosity. If we can respond in the completely opposite way, however, and be proactive in looking for areas where we may have contributed to another's resentment, we can stop situations from escalating and eventually create cultures in which resentment has little chance of taking hold.

When Simon found the courage to look at what he may have done to cause resentment, there were many signs that he had made missteps in the way he dealt with staff on a day-to-day basis. He did this both by making people feel inferior and breaking their expectations, and, in particular, undermining certain staff members with public backbiting. Little wonder, he slowly realised, that many employees felt let down or confused. He had failed to meet their expectations as a leader. He also now saw that he had been changing his expectations according to his mood, or the mood of the staff, so there had been very little consistency in his interactions. It was now unsurprising to him that some wrote on the survey that they saw him at the centre of a culture of favouritism and cronyism.

Simon confessed to feeling overwhelmed when he realised how many times he had done these things. Michael reminded him that gratitude is a 'practice', and said that every move away from his own resentment and doing something about another's was a step towards gratitude. Rather than asking him to engage with all the staff in a new way, Michael suggested that Simon choose just a few practices that he could focus on over the next few weeks. As he hadn't done anything like this before, Simon was relieved to learn that it was best to go slowly and to choose people who he felt were not too far out of his comfort zone. He needed to proceed in a step-by-step way, and it was okay to feel awkward and to not get things completely right the first couple of times.

Michael helped Simon rehearse some things he might want to say, such as: 'My frequent public put-downs about your recent car mishap must have embarrassed you, and I now want to say how sorry I am.' Or: 'I let you down when I took away the sick leave entitlement that I had promised. I broke that agreement, and I apologise unreservedly.'

Simon began to experience more and more often that things shifted for him when he started a conversation with an attitude of gratitude. However, it definitely took some preparation. With a sense of shame that he hadn't done this before, he realised he needed to get to know more about each person first and build his connection with them if his gratitude was to be sincere and meaningful.

Simon had to rehearse several times, as well as think about how he would handle any negative responses. Still feeling vulnerable and sensitive, he would have to muster his strength not to take offence. He also had to talk through with Michael his fear that he wouldn't necessarily be able to solve their problem, and that it would open up a can of worms and further complaints.

When Simon first tried to start these conversations, he could sense that the other person wanted to speak to him as little as possible, or just avoid him. When he took opportunities to speak to staff in the corridors or the tearoom, they would avoid eye contact and look at their watch or phone, offering excuses as to why they needed to get going. Based on what they had experienced in the past with Simon, they didn't trust him and still feared being mocked or dismissed or made to feel small.

Michael suggested that when Simon started conversations, he would have to learn to move past their defensiveness, distrust and insecurities and try to find a way of connecting, of relating. To do this, he needed to be in a state of preparedness – recognising in advance what he was grateful for in them and holding this in his inner attitude – in readiness for his meetings with his staff. He needed to do this if his rehearsed words of apology were to have any chance of resonating with them. Likewise, he needed to accept they might never want to talk.

Over a month or so of working with just a few people he could find at least some connection with, Simon was able to see that their demeanor shifted and they looked brighter when they came to work. One of them even started to greet Simon as he walked by his office in the mornings.

## Making it easier for others to speak to us

Having taken up this gratitude practice towards a few of his staff, and while continuing with his own personal daily gratitude practices, Simon now felt ready and resilient enough to embark on the next big step of cultural change: making it easier for others to come to him with their grievances.

Secure in Michael's support, he made a public statement saying that he really wanted to listen to how he could handle things differently and to learn from his mistakes. He invited people at all levels of the organisation to come and speak to him directly. He acknowledged that he might get it wrong, and that it could take several goes before they understood each other. He also said he couldn't promise that he would solve all their problems or give them everything they wanted but said he would do his best to listen and give proper attention to everyone's grievances.

Simon knew the stakes were high. If he betrayed the trust of those who came to see him or didn't handle the conversation in such a way that the person felt heard and respected, he knew they would go back and report this to others in their circle and their collective resentment towards him would grow even more. Simon needed to focus on dealing with everyone equitably so he wouldn't be seen as playing favourites anymore. He also had to find a way to move past his own pain at hearing things that shocked and angered him, and not bring his resentment to the situation.

When a person comes to discuss their resentment towards us, we need to be brave and prepared to experience discomfort or hardship in order to truly and attentively listen to their pain. As poet Ben Okri says, 'To listen is to suffer'.

Simon was able to recognise that others would find it just as difficult to come to him and air their grievances as he himself was fearful about it – quite likely even more difficult, as it's one of the hardest things we can do. The powerful position he had would automatically make it difficult for people to tell him about their resentment. He needed to open the conversation by saying that he understood that it took courage for the person to come to speak to him directly. He needed to say things like: 'Thank you for coming...' or 'I really appreciate your courage...' What's more, he had to mean it so it didn't come out in a condescending way.

## Becoming a great leader

Simon felt more integrity than he had ever experienced before – both in himself and with his colleagues – and started to enjoy the process of acknowledging each employee he met with in an individual way, in conversations that were often started with an apology. He'd say that he was sorry that he hadn't told them in the past that he was grateful for their contribution to the company or to their clients or fellow team members. He shared with people what he had learned from them. For those he didn't know well, he met with their line managers first to find out more about their interests and contribution.

None of this could be rehearsed. Just as we need to find ways of meaningfully expressing gratitude to another, we also need to find meaningful ways of hearing about their resentment. Simon showed that he heard them by repeating back what he believed were the main points, so he could confirm he'd understood the message. He also invited each one to come back again if they felt that they needed more time to talk. In some cases, he needed to check in the next day or a few days later to see if they were okay and that they didn't feel too exposed and vulnerable after being honest with 'the boss'.

This process was not easy, and at times was very painful. Simon had to try with all his might not to take all their grievances personally or defensively.

While this was his focus, Simon needed to delegate many of his responsibilities for several months, postpone meetings and work overtime to catch up on his core tasks. However, this became a minor inconvenience as he saw more life in the faces of those who spoke to him, as he started to be filled with gratitude for their courage and the trust they showed in him, and for their greetings and smiles in the corridors. His confidence in his capacity as a leader slowly returned. Simon was giving a strong message to everyone in the company that relationships and people matter more than getting the job done and meeting targets.

Simon had started to become not just a good leader but a great leader. A little over a year after he had received the survey responses, when he met with the CEO for his annual review, there was a marked difference in the way she welcomed him into her office and in her smile of appreciation. Simon himself smiled from deep within as she listed all the positive things she had noticed and the unsolicited good reports she had received from many of the staff he managed. He knew these must have been genuine as he had put a lot of work into creating a culture in which people were no longer afraid to give direct feedback – even though there was still a long way to go with some.

Hope had been restored. The self-resentment Simon had initially felt about what the survey had shown him had been replaced by self-gratitude for being able to go through the adversity without running away and therefore missing the immense wisdom it offered him.

And of course, we can't finish this chapter without acknowledging the immense wisdom displayed by Simon's boss, the CEO of the company. She clearly had enough insight not to resent Simon, but rather to help him through modelling that people and relationships really matter. She did this by acknowledging him as a person rather than as a collation of performance metrics, holding to a vision of change for Simon that was realistic and gradual so that it was achievable, and offering Simon the help she felt he needed to be able to make the changes. In her wisdom and grace, the CEO supported Simon even when she knew he had been undermining her. Such leadership is deeply inspiring and transformative.

## Giving time

Although placed within a company context, we can learn a lot from this story about how to deal with another's resentment towards us and the role gratitude plays as a catalyst of transformation.

We have explored many gratitude practices in this chapter, and I invite you to take up any that resonate with you in your situation. Again, this should be a situation that sits within your comfort zone. As Simon found, these practices include acknowledging our part in another's resentment, growing our resilience through self-gratitude and a state of preparedness, reflecting on whether we may have failed to meet another's expectations or made them feel inferior, looking for signs that another feels resentful towards us and addressing this with them, and creating a safe and trusting environment for the person to talk openly about any grievances they have. Although on the surface such actions may not seem like gratitude practices, they are crucial for enabling gratitude to be expressed and received in difficult relationships. As you contemplate doing any one of these practices, you are bringing your awareness to the other person and sending out a message that this relationship matters. This in itself is a huge step forward.

Sometimes people hold resentment towards us that is deep and ingrained. We may have hurt them deeply and it can take a long time to restore their trust. It may be difficult to ascertain whether or not our gratitude practices make a difference to them or address their resentment in any way. This is when we return to the maxim of gratitude: our measure of success is how we feel inside, not the response of the other person.

As Simon discovered, the gratitude practices suggested here are not always easy. It usually takes great courage and strong motivation. Simon's CEO gave him a second chance and the kind of compassion we all need when we have upset and angered others and inadvertently caused them to feel resentful. We also may well need the right kind of support, which at times may include professional help.

Another important factor highlighted in this chapter is time. Looking for quick fixes when we are trying to change entrenched behaviours does more harm than good. In Simon's story, we saw Michael supporting and managing a range of dynamics over time, including building Simon's capacity for self-gratitude, which allowed him to hear criticism, to reflect honestly on his own part in things, and to manage his self-resentment.

To make the untangling process easier, it's important that the resentful person has the courage and skills to be able to talk about their resentment with the person they feel has caused it to fester in them. In the next chapter, we will explore strategies that can help us to overcome our fear of talking about our grievances with another, and allowing them to do the same with us, and the vital role that gratitude plays in the process.

# Chapter 8

## Speaking up about our grievances

*Fear: the best way out is through.*

– Helen Keller

## The perils of speaking up

Not all of Simon's employees took up the opportunity to speak about their resentment directly with him. Some may have felt they just couldn't or were afraid of what their workmates would think if they displayed a change of heart. Some probably questioned the point of it. Like most of us, a lot of them probably grew up in environments where keeping the peace was more important than speaking up and taking the risk of creating conflict.

I need to stress at the outset that choosing not to speak directly to the person who we feel has caused us pain is not cowardly. As I have mentioned before, one gratitude practice is not necessarily better or more worthy than another. Just because there is a whole chapter on this approach doesn't mean that it is the ultimate act of gratitude or the only way to address resentment. In some cases, speaking directly may not be the best course of action.

However, there are some wounds that won't heal until they are spoken about to the person we resent, and they keep festering because the pain is stuck. We could go on putting up with the resentment for the rest of our life, but this can never be an effective way forward.

There are many resources for growing your confidence and skills in being able to communicate your grievances directly.[1,2,3] In this chapter, we will explore how gratitude can play a particular role in giving us the courage and skills to speak up in this way. While acknowledging how difficult it can be to speak directly to the person who we feel has hurt us, this chapter offers progressive steps we can put in place before we make this move. Each step is a gratitude practice that supports the untangling process of our resentment until we get to what's probably the biggest challenge of all: our fear of confronting another.

I can name many occasions in my life when I have shrunk away from speaking directly to a person whom I held resentment towards. One particular case was when I was doing my PhD and felt that my supervisor was treating me with great neglect and unfairness. At the time, the very thought of addressing this directly with him riddled me with fear, and I can still feel a knot in my stomach when I think about it. As my supervisor held all the power in our relationship, and I was sitting at the bottom of his mountain in terms of knowledge, prestige and position at the university, it felt safer to just grit my teeth and persevere rather than talk to him. I realise now that I was simply too resentful to get past the pain in order to find the right words. Resentment was robbing me of my own voice, and it has taken years to find that voice again.

When I tried to change supervisors, I was advised that this could cause further negative consequences as my actions would more than likely be looked upon by others, and the supervisor himself, as insulting. Was it the right decision to stay even though the unfair treatment kept escalating? At the time, in order to avoid the likely negative consequences, it probably was. From another angle though, I lost out badly. My resentment was sent in ugly ways as I talked about my supervisor behind his back to some of my fellow students. This probably added another year to the time it took to complete my PhD and robbed me of the joy in doing the actual research. As I said, because of how I reacted, I lost out badly.

I can see now – especially as I am a PhD supervisor myself – that my supervisor was doing the best he could while burdened with many demands, with my thesis just being one of them. In hindsight I also realise that I was coming from a position of entitlement that was likely frustrating and distasteful to him.

At the time I couldn't even see the irony in the fact that gratitude was an emerging theme in my research. The students who were my research participants were reporting that gratitude had a significant and positive impact on their ability to be engaged and connected to their subject matter. My lack of gratitude – supplanted entirely by the resentment I felt towards my supervisor – was doing the opposite in my own studies, from which I felt disengaged and disconnected. Oh, how true is the saying, 'We teach what we most need to learn.'

## Becoming aware of the ways we express our resentment

Returning to our exploration of the nature of resentment in Chapter 2, it's an emotion that remains stuck because we are shocked that the other person could behave in such a way, and we don't know how to release the underlying pain. We might also hold on to our resentment as a kind of moral stance against the perceived injustice of the action. Although it's a play on words, resentment needs to be 're-sent', but we can't let it go.

Here we return to the question posed in the title of this book: 'How can I be grateful when I feel so resentful?' In this chapter, we are going to discover that one of the keys to answering this question is to find constructive and life-enhancing ways of loosening the hold of resentment, to be able to resend it positively.

A first step in this process is to identify the *destructive* ways in which we might be processing our resentment, thinking that we are resending it, but we're really not. This generally takes two forms. The first is that we internalise it, and as such it can contribute to many of the ailments mentioned earlier in this book: ulcers, gastric disorders, heartburn, cardio-respiratory symptoms, cardiac disease, intolerance to exercise, headaches, backache, joint pain, insomnia and stress.[4]

The second destructive way in which we process our resentment is to talk negatively about the other person behind their back. In this book you would have noticed various references to 'backbiting'. We try to release our stuck resentment through words, and generally these words 'bite' and defame the other person. We engage in name-calling, gossiping, ridiculing, belittling, whingeing, blaming and being disparaging, cynical or sarcastic.

However, backbiting is often done quite unconsciously. It isn't necessarily done to deliberately hurt the other person or to get back at them. It can be the only strategy we have to process the pain and seek the support of others. At some level, we may know it's destructive, but we feel so hurt and our yearning to seek justice is so strong that we can't control it.

This way of expressing resentment becomes more prevalent when our resilience is low, our stress levels are high, or when we are busy or overworked. It's also more pervasive when it's part of the culture or everyday behaviour of those around us, or when we're part of a culture where there is little gratitude or care for relationships. As we explored in the previous chapter, it becomes the norm when a leader engages in this kind of behaviour, and it thus permeates the whole organisation.

We also need to acknowledge how difficult it can be to refrain from backbiting. Although I became aware of how much I was backbiting my supervisor, and the trail of destruction I was leaving in my path in terms of reputational damage to him and my own loss of integrity, it wasn't just a simple matter of deciding to no longer do it. No matter how much I tried, it had become a habit that was difficult to break. Moreover, my willpower was taken over by the potent sense of broken expectations I felt at his handling of the situation.

I was in a vicious cycle (a term I use a couple of times in this book because it's so pertinent), as I was being consumed by my self-resentment for behaving like this in the first place. Even though I felt I was being treated unfairly by my supervisor, I started to beat myself up for not being stronger, not being able to be grateful. I couldn't find 'perfect' Kerry in this situation, so I just gave up.

## Regaining integrity

So, what are the ways forward so that our resentment can be re-sent more constructively? An initial step would be to grow our awareness of both the behaviour arising from our resentment and its negative impact. Even if it's the norm in many contexts to bottle things up or backbite, in my humble opinion I believe it's important that we never accept it as the status quo and make such behaviours okay.

As just mentioned, though, at the same time it's important not to set up unrealistic expectations of ourselves and think that we can just stop behaving in this way. Here, it might be helpful to examine our notion of what it is to have integrity. For me, integrity isn't about always making perfect choices or never making mistakes. Integrity is about recognising when we have deviated from our desired way of being and making efforts to do it differently next time. Integrity isn't about staying on course all the time. It's a process of reflection that is about getting back on course after realising we have gone off course. From my experience, this is a continual work in progress.

How this would have looked in the situation with my supervisor is that, instead of berating myself when I recognised that I was backbiting him, I could have reflected and tried to do better the next time. Or I could have sought to remedy my negative talk by saying something positive about him when I had the opportunity. Another strategy would have been to work on creating better habits, such as deflecting the conversation when I was around others who were backbiting and was tempted to join in.

Every time we refrain from resending our hurt by bringing down another, we open the door for more gratitude to enter – not only towards the other person but also towards ourselves. On a broader scale, ideally we would be aiming for kinder environments, where trust and *reconnaissance* are the norm and where backbiting behaviour is therefore less likely to occur.

## Differences between backbiting and critical thinking

A common reason many think it's okay to backbite is because they think it's a sign of intellectual competence. Those who work in the public arena, such as politics or academia, and those who identify with being analytical, critical thinkers, are particularly prone to this way of thinking. We see it as our business to critique the current status quo. Critical thinking is often our motivation for doing the work we're doing. We're paid to find problems and suggest solutions. We hold critical thinking and skepticism as high-level and admirable skills. Indeed, we see them as a democratic right that we need to cherish and celebrate. Taking this further, many would say that it's the resentment behind some of this critical thinking that fuels action to stop the injustices in the world. The argument goes that to not give expression to this resentment would be morally unacceptable and make us apathetic and complacent. It's our resentment that gives us our spark, our edge, our burning passion to make a difference.

The problem is that debate and discussion in the Western world have sometimes been based on the idea that critique and backbiting are one and the same thing. We bring others down at the same time as we bring down their ideas.

However, it's important to realise that critique is an objective process of weighing things up or evaluating them in order to make an assessment about how to act on a certain issue. Our motivation is to find fault in ideas for the sake of reaching the truth or coming up with a better answer. Critique is directed towards *ideas*. Backbiting, on the other hand, usually arises out of resentment that is directed towards another *person*.

Gratitude and backbiting can't coexist, but gratitude and critical thinking make excellent partners. Being in a state of gratitude assists us to open our minds and hearts to what's really going on. It helps us to think more clearly and analyse more thoughtfully.[5] We can have an immense appreciation for the matter that is being analysed while at the same time assessing it and developing ideas about how it could be improved. Indeed, it's this state of appreciation that was at the source of the thinking of some famous innovators, such as Albert Einstein, who brought a sense of gratitude, awe and wonder to all his intellectual pursuits.

As I found when I was doing my PhD, I was distracted by my underlying resentment and disappointment. Rather than awakening clear thinking, my backbiting created clouds that blocked clarity and creativity.

No matter how much training in focused attention we've done or how much we've developed a strong habit to think clearly, resentment has such a strong hold at a deep level of consciousness that, where it exists, it's almost impossible to accomplish focused and positive critique. There's also a sense in which resentment suppresses our spirit, and therefore our inspiration. If we are backbiting or blaming others, we effectively separate ourselves from interconnectedness. We can damage our relationships, turning people into enemies and fuelling our antagonism to those we resent. In many organisations, this is one of the biggest obstacles to truly innovative and inspired work.

## Choosing *one* person to witness our pain

You might be reading all of this and protesting that I'm depriving you of your only way of staying sane. Debriefing or talking to your mates at the pub on a Friday night about all the grievances you have felt during the week, for example, can seem to be the best medicine for being able to get free of resentment, to let it go. It can seem like the only thing that helps to mark the end of a tough week, so that the weekend can be relaxing and the following week more palatable.

But if we reflect more deeply, we are able to see that this usually only provides temporary relief and doesn't take the resentment away. It ultimately makes us feel worse, as it solidifies our position and entangles others in our grievance by asking them to agree with us. It also stops us doing something constructive about it or acknowledging our part in what makes the relationship difficult. What's more, by doing this off-loading, we're engaging in the same kind of hurtful behaviour that we might well be accusing the other of. We're bringing them down with our words, trying to get the upper hand in ways that would certainly give them cause to feel resentful towards us if they were to hear about it.

The support we receive from others when we're backbiting may seem invaluable because it stops us from feeling alone. However, although it may appear that our friendship or connection has been strengthened through sharing our grievances, it can often backfire. If people see that you are capable of doing this to another, it's natural to conclude that you may do this to them one day. They may well be right. It likewise could damage people's trust if they observe you acting 'as sweet as pie' to the person you have slandered when you go back to work on Monday.

A more constructive way to address our resentment would be to speak about it to a trusted and competent listener, who is able to be objective and confidential and not judge the other person.

Whereas backbiting is reactive, and we give little thought to the consequences of what we are saying or who we are talking to, we are much more conscious and proactive when we deliberately choose a person to speak to about our grievances and give a stated purpose to our discussion. If we take the latter course, we are far more likely to be able to identify the cause of our resentment and find a solution. We may also come to more clearly see our part in the situation that's arisen.

The very act of speaking with this intention in mind activates a different kind of thinking compared to when we stay silent and ruminate, or blurt out our grievance without any integrity or concern about the impact. It also creates a different way of speaking, a kind that lifts us and gives us more integrity.

I also recommend to consciously choose just one person to act as our sounding board. In the words of mystic Caroline Myss, we only need 'one witness to our pain'. We don't need to keep going over and over it with whoever will listen. As we saw in the case of Madeline in Chapter 4, when she was processing the pain she felt about the ageism in her workplace, she consciously chose Leah, and only Leah, to speak to. How we establish our intention with the person we choose to share with is crucial to keeping our integrity. They may think that we're rather strange if we ask them to be a witness to our pain. However, as Madeline did with Leah, we could ask them if it's okay to confidentially discuss an issue of concern, request that they don't judge the person, acknowledge that we are only giving them our side of the story, say that the purpose is to seek understanding of the underlying issues, and share that the aim is to move past the shock and distress so that a conversation with the person becomes possible. We could also ask them for support in getting clearer about our thoughts and feelings, and to rehearse what we might say to the person we have a grievance with.

Our aim is to do this in a way that is helpful to ourselves and not damaging to others. The consciousness we bring to this process allows gratitude to thrive, and therefore each of these steps could be considered gratitude practices.

## Finding our 'why' for having the courage to speak directly

So far, we've explored the importance of recognising the consequences of backbiting another, the need to regain our integrity, and the support we can put into place to be able to do so. Our next move is to explore more deeply *why* it might be important to speak directly to the person.

It's through the act of speaking up that both we and they can become more fully aware of the nature of our resentment and its hold over us. In talking through our broken expectations or the ways in which we have been left feeling inferior, we are able to clarify boundaries and assert our values. Although this is a difficult practice, speaking up may be the only thing that can give us back our sense of justice, equity and, in the end, our peace of mind and wellness. It's also often the only way to restore the relationship.

Staying silent not only hurts us but also prevents the other person from having the opportunity to grow, consider the impact of their actions and perhaps one day feel the need to apologise. Speaking makes the unconscious conscious for both parties. Silence can often create confusion for the one we resent. They can often sense that all is not okay and are trying to make sense of our sudden change of heart, or behaviours that malign or isolate. This would very likely cause them to feel resentful towards us.

If we fail to speak up when it's appropriate to do so and continue to tolerate the behaviour, we could be seen as complicit in the actions that are hurting us. In weighing up the consequences of speaking up or not, perhaps it might motivate us if we see that if the person who has caused us harm keeps behaving in this way, they will cause further harm – not only towards us but to others. We might then feel we have the moral obligation to speak up.

Our experience of longing for a safe environment in which to speak about our pain, without fear and in total safety, can lead to us reflecting on how we can create such an environment for another so that they feel safe to come and speak to us directly. In the previous chapter, we saw how Simon discovered the power of this gratitude practice to transform workplace culture. As mentioned, the act of being willing to allow another to air their grievances with us is one of the most powerful ways to start to untangle the ball of string and create trusting environments where gratitude can thrive.

But you may ask, why do you need to speak to the person yourself? Why can't you just email them or ask someone to do it for you – a trusted friend or a colleague, perhaps? Although this could be an appropriate move when you feel in harm's way or just don't feel resilient enough to speak up, there's much to be gained by speaking directly to the person. This way, you are able to experience each other's reality. The other person gains an actual physical sense of your pain and so is more likely to be awakened to their part in it.

What's more, when we speak, we do a different kind of thinking or problem-solving than when we write about it, and certainly than when we stay silent. The act of speaking can activate a different kind of intelligence, and in this instance may provide a clarity that can help us move on rather than staying stuck.

It's helpful to be aware that there are whole countries in which people do not have the freedom to speak openly about their feelings of being wronged. If we live in a place where we are able to speak out without fear of recrimination or punishment, this basic human right is to be treasured, respected and valued. To use it powerfully and proactively is a way of expressing gratitude for being given this opportunity when so many are deprived of it.

## Redefining confrontation

I know people who have achieved amazing feats – climbing the Himalayas, recovering from three bouts of chemotherapy, single-parenting five children – but who find the idea of speaking honestly and directly to another about their resentment to be absolutely terrifying. In many of my workshops and book clubs, I hear and taste the fear that people feel when they are invited to contemplate this idea. A common refrain is, 'I would rather die than speak directly to them'. They are quick to utter the word 'confrontation'. To speak honestly is perceived as the equivalent of going into battle or entering a conflict zone, where they need armour to protect themselves.

Again, it's important to acknowledge these fears as legitimate and to let them guide us if we are feeling unsafe. However, if we let them rule us, we run the risk of not being able to move on. Elizabeth Gilbert's sage advice in *Big Magic* can be very useful in helping us to see this fear in a different way and allow it to accompany us: we need some of our fears. They play an important evolutionary role. But she reminds us that there are some that we don't need, and it's important to know the difference.

Rather than being negative about such fears, or afraid of them, she invites us to be curious, and give them a place and plenty of space in any actions that require courage. Gilbert tells these fears that they will not be making the decisions: 'You're allowed to have a seat, and you're allowed to have a voice, but you are not allowed to have a vote.'[6] We can use this wisdom to find ways of putting our fears in their rightful place, so they don't dominate our decision-making and rob us of the courage to speak out.

As well as being curious about our fears, we should also remember the role self-gratitude plays in redefining confrontation. Speaking up is an important part of self-care. It helps us to be resilient and have clear boundaries.

I can see now that I was coming from a perfection perspective in nearly everything I did while doing my PhD, and there wasn't much room for self-gratitude. If there had been, this would have given me greater confidence and a sense of self-worth, and I wouldn't have handed my personal power over to my supervisor. Then I wouldn't have been so afraid of what I perceived as his power over me. Even though it may have been tricky, this might well have given me the wisdom and confidence to look for another supervisor.

However, at the time, I equated any kind of assertiveness with rocking the boat, and I was also afraid that I would be labelled a bad person or a troublemaker. I was strongly defending my self-image as a peacemaker and a nice person (even though I wasn't being that nice behind the scenes). Scars from growing up in a family where my parents often dealt with conflict in destructive ways left me fearful of any kind of confrontation. Over the years, I've realised that I not only settled for being 'nice' but actually 'too nice' for my own good, which is a recipe for resentment about feeling inferior in the presence of those who I feel have more power than me.

Taking Elizabeth Gilbert's advice on board and developing curiosity about my fear of confrontation – even all these years later – has helped me see that there can be a healthy coexistence of both 'nice' and 'assertive' qualities. I've also realised that one does not rule out the other but that they can in fact be complementary.

If I had been more fully practising gratitude at the time of conflict with my supervisor, I could have started with *reconnaissance* and acknowledged him more as a person, rather than someone who wielded all the power in a particular role. He was and is, first and foremost, a human being. If I had centred myself more fully on what I was grateful for in him, I might have grown my empathy and been able to see the enormous pressures he was under. My fear of speaking directly to my supervisor could have been surpassed by the knowledge that, for me, the relationship between us was just as important as the task of getting my PhD done.

## The need to belong

One of the biggest fears in talking to the other person about our resentment is that we will be rejected by them and their wider circle of friends or colleagues.

As psychologist Abraham Maslow proposes, people's motivations in life can be explained by their strategies to meet certain needs.[7] In his hierarchy of needs, Maslow holds that after physical needs (such as food and shelter), people have a need for safety, and straight after that is the need for love and belonging. We can't reach the ultimate goal of self-actualisation until these needs of safety and belonging are met. If speaking honestly to someone about our resentment is a mark of self-actualisation, then perhaps the need to belong needs to be met before we can act with this kind of wisdom.

This can play out in a number of ways. As just mentioned, you may be afraid that suddenly being more open with someone about your resentment towards them may lead you to being rejected by them or a group you are part of. Or you may have felt the pressure to be the same as you always have been in order to avoid the risk of being ostracised. This could be especially problematic for someone living in a small town or community or in a workplace where people have known you for a long time and expect you to behave in a certain way. It can feel risky to choose fairly suddenly to refrain from backbiting and blaming others when you have relied upon fitting in with a group that does this often. It might make others feel that you are not part of that group anymore, or that you think you're better than they are. The need to belong wins out over the need to be kind.

I believe that in cultures or communities where *reconnaissance* is the norm, people feel a greater and truer sense of belonging, without being dominated by their need to fit in. Going back to Maslow's hierarchy, the need to belong is met by receiving *reconnaissance* from another.

## Valuing relationships

Our fear of getting something wrong in our communication with others shows us how highly relational we are at the core of our being. Instinctively, we care deeply about the safety and stability of the core relationships in our lives. It's a way of making sure we are okay.

Of course, I'm not recommending that we try to become best friends with someone we feel has hurt us. But my fundamental belief is that we care more deeply than we perhaps realise about having harmony in our relationships. Otherwise, we wouldn't be so scared about hurting the other person, or how that relationship might change, or what a damaged relationship does to us and those around us. This is why a very powerful statement at the beginning of a discussion about our resentment could be something like, 'Because our relationship matters to me...'

We can grow the sincerity behind this statement through our gratitude practices. When we look for the good in another and remember what we have received from them, we are more able to move away from a dynamic of confrontation and towards one of restoration and reconciliation. Our starting point is what they have given us, rather than what we feel they have taken away. This in itself can often soften the interaction and, as a consequence, they will be less likely to take offence. So, rather than focus on our resentment towards another, our focus is on their inherent value and worthiness.

\* \* \*

In this chapter, we have explored one of the most difficult aspects of restoring difficult relationships: speaking directly to someone about the pain they have caused us. We have learned that it's important to identify the destructive ways in which we express resentment and to then embark on gratitude practices that enable us to resend that resentment in constructive and proactive ways. We have also seen how the choices we make have a big impact on preserving our integrity, and so we need to consciously and purposefully choose the support we may need to be able process our pain. It's important to become friends with our fears and redefine our perception of confrontation so that we can see it as a positive way of starting to untangle difficult relationships. Here, self-gratitude plays an important role in reminding us to have strong boundaries and to only embark on these steps if it feels right to do so.

We have seen that it's often hard enough to speak about our pain within a familiar cultural setting. As you will discover in the following chapter, complexities magnify when we try to do this with people of a culture that is different from our own. Expanding our understanding of cross-cultural expressions of gratitude and resentment can serve to grow our empathy for those who struggle to fit in with the norms of the predominant culture, and can consequently enhance our communication skills.

# Chapter 9

# Cross-cultural differences

*Please knock before you enter.*
– Karen Martin

## Cultural contexts

So far, our exploration has taken place in a Western context. While much of the discussion of gratitude and resentment in the book would be relevant across cultures, it's important to note that some aspects of the untangling process would need to be explored further to take into account cultural differences.

In this chapter, you will read some stories outlining what I have learned as a Westerner, from either working and travelling in other countries or through my relationships with people from other cultures. To give a taste of some of the intricacies one might need to consider in cross-cultural expressions of gratitude, I discuss examples of Australian Aboriginal and Torres Strait Islander cultures, as well as the cultures of Indigenous Africans, Iranians and Chinese people. Please be aware that these are my interpretations, framed by my own cultural background, and are certainly meant to be neither cultural stereotyping nor offering a broad statement about all people from these cultures.

I have not mentioned the significant historical background of intergenerational trauma, inequality and oppression for some of the cultures we will be exploring, and the influence this has on how gratitude and resentment are felt and expressed. Neither have I gone into detail about how gender or generational differences might play out in each of the scenarios.

In exploring these stories, we can achieve two things: we can uncover some of the rich dimensions of gratitude in cultures different to our own, and we are able to learn how to be more culturally aware when giving and receiving gratitude so that this doesn't lead to a breakdown in communication. In fact, one of the best ways to build a strong relationship with someone from another culture is to deepen our understanding of how they express gratitude and resentment. We might even find that our everyday communication can break down and lead to conflict if we don't consider these differences. This alone demonstrates how crucial gratitude and resentment are to the fabric of our everyday lives.

In terms of everyday resentment, a common difficulty in speaking directly about our resentment when it involves someone from a different culture arises from the fear that we may insult them. This can be so significant that people who have migrated to another country often find they have to change their whole personality in order to fit in. It's more straightforward to hold one's tongue, to become as quiet as a mouse so as not to offend. This in turn can grow their resentment – not only because they can't express it in the way they need it to be received, but because they aren't able to express it at all.

As we have just discussed, being able to voice our resentment directly has so many complexities even within one culture. Those of us of Anglo-Saxon heritage, for example, might have grown up with a tradition of keeping the peace at any cost, having a stiff upper lip and not rocking the boat. I have often wondered if this cultural influence is why secretive backbiting and slandering others can seem acceptable in some contexts.

Such behaviour stands in stark contrast to the norms set by people of Italian or other southern European heritage, who are renowned for their ability to voice grievances openly and passionately, often without any filters whatsoever. For example, those who have had the pleasure of being absorbed in Elena Ferrante's novels might note how much the word 'resentment' is mentioned as she describes in minute detail how it plays out in the language and behaviour of the protagonists in Naples.

My first foray into researching gratitude from a cross-cultural perspective was in the context of First Nations cultures in Australia. It was through this that I was introduced to the brilliant thesis of Aboriginal scholar Karen Martin, *Please knock before you enter*.[1] Her work gave me an ethos to follow not only when conducting my research but also when trying to come to know another from any other culture. Karen Martin reminds us that our understanding of any culture is only ever our interpretation and not something we can necessarily generalise about. As she says, 'To represent our worlds is ultimately something we can only do for ourselves using our own processes to articulate our experiences, realities and understandings.'[2]

There is so much to be said about both gratitude and resentment in each of the cultures I'm about to discuss, and each deserves at least a whole chapter of its own. However, I have just tried to capture the essence of what I have interpreted as some of the important differences. I have limited the discussion about resentment to how it might be voiced to the person who we feel has caused us pain, and whether the culture makes this a given or a taboo.

## Australian Aboriginal and Torres Strait Islander cultures

First Nations cultures in Australia are highly diverse, with a presence of over 250 different language groups on mainland Australia and across Torres Strait. Each language is specific to a particular place and people and their cultural practices.

Katie, a teacher with an Anglo-Celtic Australian background, had recently started teaching in an Aboriginal community school in a remote part of Australia. Initially, she was shocked to find that she was rarely thanked by any of her students or other community members. When Katie handed back some work to a student, they would just take it and walk away. At first, she thought this was rude, but then she wondered if they didn't like her or if she had offended them.

From her experience of teaching in classrooms of students who were predominantly Western, Katie was used to building strong relationships with her students by expressing gratitude to them. When she did this in the classroom of Aboriginal children, the students would just turn their heads or walk away as if she hadn't said anything. Katie's overt expressions of gratitude weren't received well because they didn't demonstrate an understanding and sensitivity of her students' culture. It felt weird to them as they hadn't grown up with these kinds of effusive words of thanks.

It was only after several months of immersing herself in this community that Katie was able to make sense of the different ways in which they expressed gratitude. She then felt ashamed about her earlier judgment that they didn't have gratitude as part of their way of communicating, or as part of their culture. Actually, gratitude is deeply ingrained, but in a different way to how most Westerners experience it. Aboriginal cultures' gratitude is already entrenched and expressed through an appreciation and respect for interconnectedness, relationships, community and ancestors – past and present. As one Aboriginal woman told Katie, 'we don't feel gratitude for ourselves, we feel it for our whole people, and it also connects us to our ancestors'. This is completely opposite to the Western individualised experience of gratitude.

Katie discovered that the Western tradition of overt expressions of thanks was unnecessary and considered over the top or 'whitefella's business' by the community. In fact, they didn't even have a word for 'thank you' or 'gratitude' in their language.[3] It was unnecessary, because gratitude was already built into the interdependence and interconnectedness that ran through their culture. Dr Aileen Moreton-Robinson, an Australian academic and First Nations activist, describes Aboriginal ways of knowing: 'One experiences the self as part of others and that others are part of the self; this is learned through reciprocity, obligation, shared experiences, coexistence, cooperation and social memory.'[4]

For this community, this interrelationship is so much at the core of who they are that to draw attention to it through conscious expressions of gratitude would call it into question. As Karen Martin says: '... the depth of this relatedness is so powerful that it guides our lives. It is our Law...'[5] Moreover, where we tend to rely on gratitude to sustain relationships, Aboriginal cultures preserve them in other ways – such as storytelling and sharing ceremonies together. When meeting someone from another group, two questions are important: who are your people and where are you from? The stories that are relayed as an answer are important in maintaining and respecting relatedness.

For Katie to show gratitude to her students, she needed first and foremost to see them through their relationships in their community. She needed to get to know this community by doing things with them and spending time with them. She did this by asking her students to introduce her to the people who took care of them. She would go out bush with them, eat with them and find out what was important to them. It was only then that she learned the most respectful and appropriate way to express gratitude for a student – by expressing that gratitude to their particular elder.

Katie came to discover that another reason why her students didn't thank her or respond to her thanks to them was that they already had a very deep centredness about who they were and how they related – a sense of patience, steadfastness and resilience acquired through their upbringing in such a strong community.

Over time, Katie also discovered something quite profound about how resentment was dealt with by this community. If a student was feeling belittled by their teacher, for example, they would talk this over with the elder responsible for them. This elder would then go directly to the school with the child to discuss the matter with the teacher. The child had to be present so that they could be educated in how to deal with such a situation with respect and by obeying the customs of their community. From when they are born, an Aboriginal child from this community is seen as a future elder and is therefore never excluded from any situation where they could be learning from an elder.

## Indigenous Africa

I had the privilege of spending time as a visiting scholar in South Africa at the invitation of a Zulu academic, Zikomo. It was here that I learned that although rituals of gratitude are important to our everyday relationships in the West, in comparison with Zulu culture we are quite impoverished in the ways we commonly express gratitude. I also learned that although there are similarities in indigenous cultures – the sense of interdependence and importance of relationships, for example – there are also important differences. It would be a huge mistake to generalise across all indigenous cultures. Also, as was just mentioned in the case of Aboriginal and Torres Strait Islander cultures, there are a great many cultural nuances that are particular to each tribe within African indigenous cultures. Moreover, some of these groups choose not to be identified as 'indigenous', which they see as a restrictive modern category.

Zikomo invited me to take a long journey to his village on the border of Zimbabwe, and to meet his father. On the way, he relayed numerous stories and folklore about gratitude in the Zulu culture, and I discovered that there are many, many rituals and symbols through which gratitude is expressed. For example, there are certain days on which one expresses gratitude for one's deceased relatives, and particular ways that children express gratitude to their parents.

There are hundreds of stories, fables and myths – mostly passed down orally – that have expressions of gratitude as their main message.

When we arrived at Zikomo's home, I noticed that although many of the surrounding houses were very basic and run-down, his father's home was relatively new and well built. There was also a shiny new car parked in the driveway. On our journey back, I learned that Zikomo gave part of his wage to support his extended family. When he first started as an academic, the university gave him a new car as part of his contract, and he immediately gave that car to his father. He did these things as a mark of gratitude to his father. Although he has four children of his own and has to catch two trains and then take a long, hot walk up a steep hill to his office, Zikomo undergoes this daily hardship with a heart full of gratitude to his father.

I was incredibly moved, but also initially a little shocked. This all made sense to me as I came to learn more about how gratitude is central to *ubuntu* – a precept that has its origins in South Africa but which has come to guide African indigenous cultures more broadly.[6] Generally speaking, the term *ubuntu* means *umuntu ngumuntu ngabuntu*, 'a person is a person through other people'.[7] You and I are so interconnected that any gratitude I feel is already inherently an expression of gratitude towards you. *Ubuntu* is based on a 'humble togetherness' and the values of intense humanness, caring, sharing, respect, compassion and other associated values. Concern for the other over and above oneself is central.

As Zikomo explained, expressions of gratitude are so important to keeping *ubuntu* alive in everyday interactions that without them one would be judged as uncivilised. In fact, in traditional tribal contexts they are what sustains the whole village.

As with First Nations Australian cultures, relationships are the starting point for gratitude, not one's individual feelings. However, one of the key points of difference between the two contexts is that in indigenous African expressions, there is much more of a need to abide by the many rituals that revolve around gratitude. As part of *ubuntu*, one demonstrates one's culture, success, character, civility and refinement through expressions of gratitude.

According to Zulu culture, one needs to lose something in the giving, to have some sense of personal sacrifice, in order for it to be a true expression of gratitude. So, people of this culture don't just give according to what is comfortable, as that wouldn't be considered real gratitude. This doesn't mean that everyone would go to the extreme of giving their parent a car, for example, or make it so demonstrative. It's the heart behind the gift that really matters. A person from this culture would be thankful for whatever another has done as an expression of gratitude because they are looking at where this gift comes from. Does it have a pure intention to make the other person happy without wanting something in return? If not, such a gift is deemed uncivilised.

No matter the gift, the best way to show gratitude is to do well, to use the gift to be a better person. How you give or receive gratitude is linked to your character and, therefore, your success. A common expression of gratitude is to help the poor and those who have less than you. If you do that, the whole community will respect you. A person who offers gratitude sincerely is accorded the honour of being seen by others as a person of great culture, a great role model. Expressions of gratitude are therefore how indigenous Africans build their character, their reputation and their standing in the community.

In Zulu culture, resentment is not tolerated nearly as much as it is in the West and is moderated by many rituals that assist in identifying it and doing something to address it. It's typically viewed as an expression of evil, an uncivilised force. As Zikomo describes it: 'Resentment, in my culture, will be a person who we'll say is evil-hearted.' When someone notices resentment in another, they feel responsibility to do something about it to rid them of it. Zikomo gave the example of when a couple is experiencing resentment and conflict in their marriage, the elderly people in their community will notice this and tell them to go and live separately for some time.

In the West, resentment is usually felt on a very personal and individual level and seen as being the responsibility of the individual to do something about. In Zikomo's culture, it is the responsibility of the whole community to address the toxic behaviour of resentment. Moreover, if the person holds on to resentment or expresses it in negative ways, this is repelled by the whole of their society. In Zulu culture, to respond to resentment in a civilised, proactive way would be seen as a measure of a good person and a measure of success – defined by Zikomo as 'being content with life'.

## Iran

Mina was a research student from Iran whom I met at a workshop I was facilitating at my university. She had been having immense problems with her supervisors and was drawn to the topic of the workshop: 'Improving relationships between supervisors and students through the practice of gratitude'. During the workshop, I could sense that Mina was uneasy and confused when she heard how grateful other students were for the smooth communication they had with their supervisors. She approached me afterwards to discuss her difficulties in private.

First of all, Mina talked effusively about how gratitude is a very important way for people in Iran to express their spirituality. In fact, it's the way they greet each other. When they ask, 'How are you?' the answer always starts with 'Thanks to God, I am in good health.'

Mina was doubtful that gratitude had any part to play in the Australian research setting. She passionately relayed her experiences of expressing gratitude to her supervisor by bringing her presents when she first arrived in Australia, saying that this is traditionally how gratitude is expressed in Iran, and particularly to those who have a high status such as university professors. To not do this would be considered rude, and she also really wanted to show this supervisor how grateful she was for taking her on as her student.

However, Mina was offended and downhearted when the supervisor told her that she didn't want any presents. Her supervisor also asked her to stop thanking her so much in her emails. She said that she didn't need her thanks as she was just doing her job. Mina found this to be cold-hearted. She had all this gratitude she needed to pour out, but there was nowhere for it to go.

Mina also started to have problems with the way the supervisor was directing her in her topic of research, and how she didn't seem to take the necessary time to understand Mina's specific interests and desired research focus. However, in Iran, a student would never question the supervisor. This would be considered a total insult, and the relationship would be severed or put in jeopardy. Mina was so afraid of speaking up, fearing that she would lose her scholarship or even get kicked out of the country. She kept working on a project that she wasn't at all interested in, as she believed she had to do exactly what her supervisor wanted. Although she became increasingly stressed about the situation and the direction her research was going in, Mina's fear of questioning authority gave her the impression there were no other options.

In our conversation, it became clear that in Iran people would not be allowed to voice their resentment directly to the person. They would instead cut off the relationship altogether. Mina relayed the example of how this had happened recently with her mother, who had been happily working for a company for the past 30 years and had one month to go before retirement. In that month, she experienced bullying and was overlooked by several of her colleagues. Rather than addressing this with them, she just left abruptly.

Mina wanted to know more about the strategies of expressing resentment proactively that we had discussed in the workshop. She was greatly relieved to know that there were ways she could start to untangle things, steps she could take so that she could speak to her supervisor about her concerns without any of the negative consequences she had imagined.

## China

My understanding of nuances in the way gratitude and resentment are expressed in Chinese culture has arisen from discussions with my students from mainland China. One of these was a pre-service teacher, Yu Yan, who went on to teach Chinese in an Australian high school. Part of her job at the school was to offer pastoral care and language support to international students in the boarding house.

When she first started teaching there, she was concerned by the many requests she had from a number of staff to help the students from mainland China to be more polite in the way they interacted with others, particularly when showing their thanks. Yu Yan was shocked, because compared to many of the Western students she was teaching, she had thought that most of these students were extremely polite. However, they were being judged because of one big difference: they didn't voice their gratitude.

Parents in mainland China generally do not expect their children to express gratitude to them. Studying hard to achieve top results is the all-important goal, so parents simply want their children to focus on this and not worry about acknowledging them. Moreover, if young people were to thank their parents or close friends, it would seem unnecessary and 'too cheesy'. To do so could make those they are thanking feel they are being treated like a stranger, as expressing gratitude is unnecessary in close relationships.

As China is a collectivist society, gratitude is considered to be part of the fabric of the culture rather than something that needs to be overtly expressed. Many Chinese people find the Western way of expressing gratitude awkward, and they struggle to know how to receive it and how to express it in return. They also feel that they risk a loss of face among their peers if they try to engage in Western expressions of gratitude.

This is one of the main reasons why Chinese international students may not thank their teachers in the way the teachers are accustomed to receiving thanks. Even if they wanted to express gratitude, many Chinese students do not know how to do this in a Western way. Similarly, when a teacher thanks them, they do not know how to respond and may need to learn culturally appropriate ways of doing this – through smiling or thanking the teacher for their acknowledgment.

Does this mean that Chinese people are lacking in gratitude? Not by any means. Gratitude is felt inwardly and expressed in different ways. There are so many wonderful examples of unspoken gratitude, most especially expressed through the medium of offering special meals. Words may not be articulated, but actions that convey gratitude are important and ever-present. In the case of gratitude to parents, this is the cornerstone of filial piety, where the child shows gratitude through respect and commitment to care for their parents. Again, in an education context, they would express gratitude by doing well in their studies and aiming for excellence in their assignments.

Yu Yan was gradually able to educate her students about typical ways of giving and receiving gratitude in a Western context by using the example of expressing gratitude to the chef who cooked them delicious meals every day. She helped her students to rehearse the words they could use to express gratitude, and to repeat these until they felt comfortable. Thanking the chef is not a common practice in mainland China and a chef would never expect thanks from diners in their restaurant. As mentioned, both the giver and receiver of spoken words of thanks in mainland China would feel awkward.

Yet a boarding-school chef in Australia who never heard words of thanks could eventually become unmotivated or lose heart, or in this case, feel resentful towards the students. Once the students started to express gratitude to the chef, they noticed that he was happier and smiled at them more. This in turn helped them understand what a difference such a simple gesture made to their connection with him, and to others in the school, when they expressed gratitude.

Yu Yan told me that one of her biggest struggles when she was at university in Australia was going to the teacher to ask for her work to be regraded, or to discuss any other grievances if she felt she was being treated unfairly. In mainland China, the channels for communication are clearly set with regards to who to speak to about your grievances – you would never talk directly to your elders or someone in a position of power or higher status. Yu Yan found it difficult to know how to approach the situation, and her biggest fear was that if she spoke directly to her teacher, it would cause disharmony. If she were in China, her fear would also be of losing face and that any confrontation would bring shame on her family.

Her culture's approach to resolving grievances is to find a diplomatic way of asking the person about the problem, rather than confronting them directly. They try to find a creative way around the issue in order to get the result they are after. In this case, Yu Yan asked the tutor many questions to get feedback rather than speaking directly about being upset about her mark.

In China, there is a high value placed on harmony in relationships, and confrontation is seen as damaging to that harmony. The relationships between employer and employee, parent and child, and husband and wife are built on centuries of tradition in which respect is characterised by agreement – even if this agreement is underpinned by resentment. To speak directly to the person who caused resentment would generate a fear of breaking the solid foundation and certainly cause one to lose face, not only with the person to whom one is speaking but with the whole society. It could result in losing status or, indeed, one's position in society.

This is reflected in a famous Chinese saying, which translates as: 'One should make a significant issue small and make a small issue disappear,' or 'Try first to make the issue sound less serious and then to reduce it to nothing at all.'

## Gratitude for difference

In this chapter, we have explored some examples of cultural differences in the way gratitude and resentment are expressed and the implications for our own enriched understanding, and we have developed an enhanced awareness of the importance of this for our everyday communication. Again, I want to emphasise that this is a limited range of individual instances, offered with the purpose of inviting inquiry into the impact of different cultural contexts. As we can see, a respectful way of 'knocking before you enter' when communicating with someone from another culture would be to tactfully seek an understanding of how they express gratitude and how they deal with resentment. Through welcoming and learning from the differences, we can avoid unconsciously expecting people to abide by our cultural norms and resenting them for not behaving in the way we expect.

We can gain a deeper understanding of our own gratitude when we see it in contrast with its expression in another culture. We can see where it's rich and where it could be further enriched by learning about the myriad other ways in which our gratitude can be expressed. This doesn't mean that we need to adopt another's way of expressing gratitude if it feels foreign to our way of being. In many cases, to do so would not only feel strange to us but also to the person from the other culture. However, cross-cultural awareness is crucial for smooth communication. It can enhance our practice of expressing gratitude in meaningful and sincere ways.

# Chapter 10

# Little actions, big effects

*In a gentle way, you can shake the world.*
— Mahatma Gandhi

My deeper understanding of the nature of resentment has helped me to see that overcoming it is one of our greatest and most important challenges as human beings. However, there's also a strong drive in us to seek justice for perceived wrongs, and this is what gives us our moral compass when it comes to how we like to be treated and how we expect others to be treated as well. As much as we want resentment to be eradicated from our lives or to live in a resentment-free world, it's difficult to imagine it because of the inequities we live with every day. What we can have, though, and what I hope this book has offered, is a different perspective on resentment, as well as strategies for working with it so that it doesn't take hold as deeply, or for as long, or as destructively in our lives. I feel that the best and perhaps the only way to achieve this is to find authentic gratitude and practise it wherever we can.

---

A question I am often asked is whether or not resentment is ever okay. Radical as it may seem, given my statement that it seems to be an integral part of us, my answer is that it is not, and we should do everything in our power to create cultures in which resentment is unable to take root. This means committing to changing the way we think about resentment in ourselves and in the environments where we live, work and play.

However, resentment is something that we can learn from – that we must learn from. In this way, injustices in our lives can be constructively addressed through being able to speak our truth. Part of that learning process is to be able to identify where resentment lies within us, to seek out its causes and to make different choices about how we are going to respond. Gratitude has a particular role to play in reminding us that such a choice is not only possible but imperative if we are to recover an essential part of our agency and our sense of interconnectedness. If we choose to turn our attention to what we are grateful for in the other person, we are able to start to loosen the hold of resentment. Paradoxically, resentment from another can hold up a mirror to show us where we have resentment towards that person, or someone else in our lives. The quickest way to start the untangling process is to reflect first on what we can change.

When we harbour grudges, and when we allow feelings of anger or disappointment to fester in our hearts, we put ourselves in the situation Nelson Mandela describes when he says, 'Resentment is like drinking poison and then hoping it will kill your enemies.' Making it okay to hold onto resentment poisons our health, our relationships, our environment and society at large. Making it okay also makes it impossible for gratitude to thrive and fulfil its life-enhancing role in helping relationships flourish, and mending them when they are broken.

If you have come to the end of this book and feel you have a long way to go, you're not alone. I've been researching this topic for over 25 years, but I still have some lingering feelings of resentment, and I still have relationships in which it's difficult to find gratitude or I can sense another's resentment towards me. I realise this when I feel tight in my stomach at hearing a certain person's name, or I find myself avoiding a gathering because a particular person will be there, or I easily join in with a backbiting conversation. I then become aware that I've only untangled part of my ball of string.

The main difference now is that when I realise I still have resentment, it doesn't have the same effect that it used to – the feelings of failure, self-judgment and shame at not being able to move on. This is progress. As I said at the beginning of this chapter, overcoming our resentment is one of our biggest challenges.

Our resentment often results in us waiting for others to mend the relationship or make the first move towards reconciliation. However, our inner peace and peaceful coexistence with others is more easily achieved if we are able to address the resentment another has towards us. This is why one of the most powerful actions we can take is to unjudgmentally reflect on three questions at the end of our day: Have I broken someone's expectations in some way? Have I made someone feel inferior? If so, how can I address this tomorrow?

Facing up to the part we have played in allowing relationships to deteriorate or become toxic can eventually free us up and allow us to move towards a new approach based on gratitude.

We need to resist the temptation to see gratitude as a quick fix. It's important to see it as a *practice*, and therefore something that we aren't going to get right all the time and that can only happen over time. A practice is something we can pick up where we got stuck and try again, using the learning gained along the way and the encouragement we feel from situations where we have been able to achieve our goals. The advantage of making it a *gratitude* practice is that it leads us to focus on the higher part of ourselves and our commitment to better relationships, rather than the details and pain of the resentment. We remember the good in ourselves, the good we have received from others and from life itself.

So, to recap: to take up gratitude as a practice, it's helpful to focus on *one* relationship at a time, *one* gratitude practice at a time, choosing a gratitude practice that is both authentic and achievable. Additionally, self-gratitude is crucial for discerning how much we can give to another at any particular time, keeping clear boundaries around the steps we feel able to take in addressing our resentment. We may need to begin by focusing on those areas of life where gratitude is easy and fill our being with gratitude for them first. This will help to build our resilience.

We can increase our confidence and skills by choosing to work on a relationship that is just a little out of our comfort zone. This grows our capacity and confidence so that when we're ready, we're able to work on untangling the more challenging relationships. We choose a gratitude practice that is challenging enough but doesn't stretch us so much that we feel defeated and just give up. Working with the principle that 'how we do one thing is how we do everything', we might well experience that just one practice with one person has a ripple effect on other, more difficult relationships, and on other aspects of our lives.

As we have discovered over the course of this book, some of the practices are focused on finding gratitude within ourselves first. These include: finding our 'why' and forming an intention for doing this work; being conscious of both what we give and receive in developing our inner attitude; ensuring that we are expressing gratitude without expecting anything in return; recognising that we can choose our perspective; developing our inner attitude of gratitude by holding a state of preparedness prior to challenging situations; and, very importantly, cultivating self-gratitude. These practices are foundational and help us to remain sincere and authentic, to maintain clear boundaries, and to develop our indicators as to which practices are going to serve us well and which we should leave until the timing is right or when we have the right kind of support. They provide the bedrock for achieving the other purpose of gratitude – social transformation: expressing gratitude to another through action.

A core principle of this book is that gratitude, by nature, is highly relational. We awaken to what we have received from another and from life itself. We are motivated to give back in ways that are not necessarily reciprocal. In these pages, we have explored some relational gratitude practices that are very powerful for untangling our resentment. These include: identifying resentment and its underlying causes; growing our empathy and compassion; practising *reconnaissance* by recognising the value of another; expressing gratitude in ways that are meaningful to the other person; becoming skilled at receiving gratitude from another; finding respectful ways to voice our resentment to another and making it easier for them to do so with us; and respecting cross-cultural differences in the ways gratitude and resentment are expressed.

Know this, though: no matter where we start when trying to untangle our difficult relationships, as long as we do start and keep going, all of our expressions of gratitude will have a positive impact, often in ways we may never know about or may only find out about years later.

Many of the gratitude practices explored in this book orient us towards improving our character. For me, this is where our true wealth lies, and it's the greatest investment we can make of our time and energy. Instead of seeing our character as fixed, echoed in statements such as, 'This is who I am and I am not going to change', we look for opportunities to change ourselves for the better. In doing so, we are giving others the freedom and encouragement to do the same. We welcome the challenges that come along with starting to address resentment in our relationships, as it's often at these times that we find wisdom in ourselves and others. It's here we can find gratitude for our resentment.

The development of our character is shaped by the choices we make to face adversity head on or try to avoid it. Trying to address the resentment we feel from difficult relationships is perhaps the greatest test of all, and therefore presents the greatest opportunity for self-growth.

When we choose to approach difficult relationships with an inner attitude of gratitude, we instinctively activate other aspects of our character without necessarily being conscious of it. As the ancient Roman statesman Cicero wrote, 'Gratitude is not only the greatest of virtues, but the parent of all others'. We have learned from stories relayed in this book that when we consciously seek to move from resentment towards gratitude, we bring forth our courage, humility, sincerity, generosity, interconnectedness, empathy, acceptance, integrity, self-regard and patience.

If we place a high priority on developing our character, we can see that working with the interplay of gratitude and resentment is an integral part of this process. But again, it's important to mention that our gratitude practices need to be done in a way that's authentic to us. Each step we take is self-defining. Through consciously choosing to pick up our ball of string and start the untangling process, we can enrich ourselves as well as the relationships we have previously found difficult or impossible.

In a world of increasing complexity, where it's easy to feel overwhelmed by fear, powerlessness and loss, we can focus on the touchstone Victor Frankl offers as 'the last of the human freedoms': our capacity to choose our attitude. I believe that choosing to see our difficulties as opportunities for growth, looking for the learning in the resentment and practising gratitude whenever and wherever we can offer the best way forward for our own peace and, ultimately, the peace and welfare of humankind.

# Acknowledgments

This book has been greatly enriched by many years of listening to participants in my workshops, university classes, book clubs and research projects, as well as many conversations with friends and strangers on planes. I am most grateful to you all for your questions and insights, and for sharing your stories.

I'd like to acknowledge the many spiritual teachers, philosophers and gratitude researchers whose dedication and insight have greatly helped me to strengthen my grasp of the meaning and relevance of this giant of a virtue.

My deep gratitude to all who have extended their friendship to read and offer suggestions on chapters and versions of this book: Christine Thambipillai, Peter O'Connor, Therese Smith, Chris Adams, Jean Pelser and Rikki Mawad. Gratitude is also greatly owed for the professional editing advice at various stages from Perri Wain, Lee Buchanan, Gina Mercer, Chris Adams, Janet Hutchinson, Virginia Lloyd and Lucy Risdale. I would particularly like to thank Jo Lucas, who so perceptively and generously read the final version with me.

To my loving partner Lynden – we make such a wonderful team. Thank you for your brilliant proofreading skills and your wordsmithing, as well as your tireless devotion and support.

My long-time friend Mike Levy, thank you so much for your encouragement and insights at various stages along the way. You really helped give shape to this book when it needed it most.

I would also like to thank Michael Leunig for his generosity in providing the image for the front cover of this book. Thank you, Michael, for inspiring us to remember gratitude for the simple things in life through your brilliant life's work as a poet, painter, cartoonist and writer.

To my precious daughter Amrita, without you the writing of this book would not have been possible. Thank you for teaching me so much about the importance of authentic and honest relationships.

My deepest thanks to all of my family, friends and loved ones for your nurturing presence in my life.

# References

## Chapter 1: Why gratitude?

1   RC Roberts, 'The blessings of gratitude: A conceptual analysis', in
    RA Emmons & ME McCullough (eds), *The Psychology of Gratitude*,
    Oxford University Press, 2004, p. 65.

2   SB Algoe, J Haidt & SL Gable, 'Beyond reciprocity: Gratitude and
    relationships in everyday life', *Emotion*, vol. 8, no. 3, 2008,
    pp. 425–429.

3   MY Bartlett, P Condon, J Cruz, J Baumann & D Desteno,
    'Gratitude: Prompting behaviours that build relationships',
    *Cognition and Emotion*, vol. 26, no. 1, 2012, pp. 2–13.

4   MY Bartlett & D DeSteno, 'Gratitude and prosocial behavior:
    Helping when it costs you', *Psychological Science*, vol. 17, no. 4, 2006,
    pp. 319–325.

5   JJ Froh, G Bono & R Emmons, 'Beyond grateful is beyond good
    manners: Gratitude and motivation to contribute to society among
    early adolescents', *Motivation and Emotion*, vol. 34, 2010,
    pp. 144–157.

6   J Tsang, 'Gratitude and prosocial behaviour: An experimental test of
    gratitude', *Cognition & Emotion*, vol. 20, no. 1, 2006, pp. 138–148.

7   G Simmel, 'Faithfulness and gratitude', in AE Komter (ed), *The Gift:
    An interdisciplinary perspective*, Amsterdam University Press, 1996,
    pp. 39–48.

8   PC Watkins & D McCurrach, 'Exploring how gratitude trains cognitive processes important to well-being', in D Carr (ed), *Perspectives on Gratitude: An interdisciplinary approach*, Routledge, 2016, pp. 27–40.

9   ibid.

10  PC Watkins, *Gratitude and the Good Life: Toward a psychology of appreciation*, Springer, New York, 2014.

11  K Howells, 'An exploration of the role of gratitude in enhancing teacher–student relationships', *Teaching and Teacher Education*, vol. 42, 2014, pp. 58–67.

12  K Howells & J Cumming, 'Exploring the role of gratitude in the professional experience of pre-service teachers', *Teaching Education*, vol. 23, no. 1, 2012, pp. 71–88.

13  M Aparicio, C Centeno, CA Robinson & M Arantzamendi, 'Gratitude between patients and their families and health professionals: A scoping review', *Journal of Nursing Management*, vol. 27, no. 2, 2019, pp. 286–300.

14  P Kini, YJ Wong, S McInnis, N Gabana & J Brown, 'The effects of gratitude expression on neural activity', *NeuroImage*, vol. 128, 2016, pp. 1–10.

15  A Otto, EC Szczesny, EC Soriano, J-P Laurenceau & SD Siegel, 'Effects of a randomized gratitude intervention on death-related fear of recurrence in breast cancer survivors', *Health Psychology*, vol. 35, no. 12, 2016, pp. 1320–1328.

16  LL Vernon, JM Dillon & ARW Steiner, 'Proactive coping, gratitude, and posttraumatic stress disorder in college women', *Anxiety, Stress & Coping: An international journal*, vol. 22, no. 1, 2009, pp. 17–127.

17  TB Kashdan, G Uswatte & T Julian, 'Gratitude and hedonic and eudaimonic well-being in Vietnam war veterans', *Behaviour Research and Therapy*, vol. 44, no. 2, 2006, pp. 177–199.

18  J Vieselmeyer, J Holguin & AH Mezulis, 'The role of resilience and gratitude in posttraumatic stress and growth following a campus shooting', *Psychological Trauma Theory Research Practice and Policy*, vol. 9, no. 1, 2017, pp. 62–69.

19  Y Israel-Cohen, F Uzefovsky, G Kashy-Rosenbaum & O Kaplan, 'Gratitude and PTSD symptoms among Israeli youth exposed to missile attacks: Examining the mediation of positive and negative affect and life satisfaction', *The Journal of Positive Psychology*, vol. 10, no. 2, 2015, pp. 99–106.

20  ME McCullough, RA Emmons & J-A Tsang, 'The grateful disposition: A conceptual and empirical topography', *Journal of Personality and Social Psychology*, vol. 82, no. 1, 2002, pp. 112–127.

21  N Petrocchi & A Couyoumdjian, 'The impact of gratitude on depression and anxiety: The mediating role of criticizing, attacking, and reassuring the self', *Self and Identity*, vol. 15, no. 2, 2016, pp. 191–205.

22  *Greater Good Magazine: Science-based insights for a meaningful life*, viewed 23 June 2021, <greatergood.berkeley.edu>.

23  CN Armenta, MM Fritz & S Lyubomirsky, 'Functions of positive emotions: Gratitude as a motivator of self-improvement and positive change', *Emotion Review*, vol. 9, no. 3, 2017, pp. 183–190.

24  PC Watkins, 2014, op. cit.

25  AM Wood, S Joseph, & PA Linley, 'Coping style as a psychological resource of grateful people', *Journal of Social and Clinical Psychology*, vol. 26, no. 9, 2007, pp. 1076–1093.

26  BL Fredrickson, 'Gratitude, like other positive emotions, broadens and builds', in RA Emmons & ME McCullough (eds), *The Psychology of Gratitude*, Oxford University Press, 2004, pp. 145–166.

27  D Martín Moruno, 'On resentment: Past and present of an emotion', in B Fantini, D Martín Moruno & J Moscoso (eds), *On Resentment: Past and present*, Cambridge Scholars Publishing, Newcastle-upon-Tyne, 2013, pp. 1–18.

28  P León-Sanz, 'Resentment in psychosomatic pathology (1939–1960)', in B Fantini, D Martín Moruno & J Moscoso (eds), *On Resentment: Past and present*, Cambridge Scholars Publishing, Newcastle-upon-Tyne, 2013, pp. 150–160.

29  AH Harris & CE Thoresen, 'Forgiveness, unforgiveness, health, and disease', in EL Worthington (ed), *Handbook of Forgiveness*, Routledge, 2005, pp. 321–333.

30  E Ricciardi, G Rota, L Sanil, C Gentili, A Gaglianese, M Guazzelli & P Pietrini, 'How the brain heals emotional wounds: The functional neuroanatomy of forgiveness', *Frontiers in Human Neuroscience*, vol. 7, article 839, 2013.

31  ES Epel, 'Psychological and metabolic stress: A recipe for accelerated cellular aging?', *Hormones (Athens, Greece)*, vol. 8, no. 1, 2009, pp. 7–22.

32  'Rumination', *Merriam-Webster.com Medical Dictionary*, Merriam-Webster, viewed 23 June 2021, <merriam-webster.com/medical/rumination>.

33  L Baider & AK De-Nour, 'Psychological distress and intrusive thoughts in cancer patients', *The Journal of Nervous and Mental Disease*, vol. 185, no. 5, 1997, pp. 346–348.

34  L Johnson, *Teaching Outside the Box: How to grab your students by their brains*, Jossey-Bass, San Francisco, 2005.

## Chapter 2: Identifying our resentment

1   J Bernal, 'Repressing resentment: Marriage, illness and the disturbing experience of care', in B Fantini, D Martín Moruno & J Moscoso (eds), *On Resentment: Past and present*, Cambridge Scholars Publishing, Newcastle-upon-Tyne, 2013, pp. 169–187.

2   A Oksenberg Rorty, 'The dramas of resentment', *The Yale Review*, vol. 88, no. 3, 2000, pp.89–100.

3   'Resent', *Online Etymology Dictionary*, viewed 23 June 2021, <etymonline.com/word/resent>.

4   WD TenHouten, 'From ressentiment to resentment as a tertiary emotion', *Review of European Studies*, vol. 10, no. 4, 2018, pp. 49–64.

5   MC Nussbaum, *Anger and Forgiveness: Resentment, generosity, justice*, Oxford University Press, 2016.

6   M Congdon, 'Creative resentments: The role of emotions in moral change', *The Philosophical Quarterly*, vol. 68, no. 273, 2018, pp. 739–757.

7   C Aggar, S Ronaldson & ID Cameron, 'Self-esteem in carers of frail older people: Resentment predicts anxiety and depression', *Aging & Mental Health*, vol. 15, no. 6, 2011, pp. 671–678.

8   GM Williamson, K Martin-Cook, M Weiner, DA Svetlik, K Saine, LS Hynan, WK Dooley & R Schulz, 'Caregiver resentment: Explaining why care recipients exhibit problem behavior', *Rehabilitation Psychology*, vol. 50, no. 3, 2005, pp. 215–223.

9   M Aparicio, op. cit.

10  RC Roberts, op. cit., p. 66.

11  ibid., p. 67.

12  K Howells, *Gratitude in Education: A radical view*, Springer, 2012.

13  K Howells, 'The transformative power of gratitude in education', in B Shelley, K te Riele, N Brown & T Crellin (eds), *Harnessing the Transformative Power of Education*, Brill Sense, 2019, pp. 180–196.

14  K Howells, 'Developing gratitude as a practice for teachers', in JRH Tudge & L Freitas (eds), *Developing Gratitude in Children and Adolescents*, Cambridge University Press, 2018, pp. 240–261.

## Chapter 3: Broken expectations

1   M Buber, *I and Thou*, trans. RG Smith, Scribner Classics, New York, 1958.

2   R Carson, *Silent Spring*, Houghton Mifflin, Boston, 2002.

3   S Baron-Cohen, *Zero Degrees of Empathy: A new theory of human cruelty*, Allen Lane, London, 2011, p. 5.

4   ibid., pp. 5–6.

5   RC Roberts, op. cit., p. 65.

## Chapter 4: A sense of inferiority

1   WD TenHouten, op. cit.

2   World Health Organization, *Global Report on Ageism*, 2021.

3   M Ure, 'Resentment/Ressentiment', *Constellations*, vol. 22, no. 4, 2015, pp. 599–613.

4   M Visser, *The Gift of Thanks: The roots and rituals of gratitude*, Houghton Mifflin Harcourt, 2009, p. 389.

5   ibid., p. 389.

6   Ditch the Label, *The Annual Bullying Survey 2016*, 2016.

7   Visser, op. cit., p. 291.

8   P Coelho, *Veronika Decides to Die*. Harper Collins, London, 2004.

## Chapter 5: Choosing an inner attitude of gratitude

1   V Frankl, *Man's Search for Meaning: An introduction to logotherapy*. Simon & Schuster, New York, 1984, p. 131.

2   K Howells, 2012, op. cit.

3   M Visser, op. cit., p. 174.

4   R Stewart, AT Kozak, LM Tingley, JM Goddard, EM Blake &
    WA Cassel, 'Adult sibling relationships: Validation of a typology',
    *Personal Relationships*, vol. 8, no. 3, 2020, pp. 299–324.

5   K Howells, 2012, op. cit.

6   K Howells, 2018, op. cit.

7   K Howells, 2014, op. cit.

8   K Howells, K Stafford, RM Guijt & MC Breadmore, 'The role of
    gratitude in enhancing the relationship between doctoral research
    students and their supervisors', *Teaching in Higher Education*,
    vol. 22, no. 6, 2017, pp. 1–18.

9   A Oksenberg Rorty, op. cit.

## Chapter 7: Addressing another's resentment towards us

1   BA Arnout & AA Almoeid, 'A structural model relating gratitude,
    resilience, psychological well-being and creativity among
    psychological counsellors', *Counselling and Psychotherapy Research*,
    2020, pp. 1–20.

## Chapter 8: Speaking up about our grievances

1   M Rosenberg, *Nonviolent Communication: A language of life*,
    PuddleDancer Press, Encinitas, CA, 2003.

2   R Kegan & LL Lahey, *How the Way We Talk Can Change the Way
    We Work: Seven languages for transformation*. Jossey-Bass, San
    Francisco, 2001.

3   KD Patterson, J Grenny, D Maxfield, R McMillan, & AI Switzler,
    *Crucial Accountability: Tools for resolving violated expectations,
    broken commitments, and bad behavior*, McGraw-Hill Education,
    New York, 2013.

4   P León-Sanz, op. cit.

5   K Howells, *How Thanking Awakens Our Thinking*, TEDx
    Launceston, 2013.

6   E Gilbert, *Big Magic: Creative living beyond fear*, Riverhead Books, New York, 2015, p. 26.

7   AH Maslow, 'A theory of human motivation', *Psychological Review*, vol. 50, no. 4, 1943, pp. 370–396.

## Chapter 9: Cross-cultural differences

1   KL Martin, *Please Knock Before You Enter: Aboriginal regulation of outsiders and the implications for researchers*, Post Pressed, Teneriffe, Qld., 2008.

2   ibid., p. 12.

3   M Visser, op. cit., p. 16.

4   KL Martin, op. cit., p. 76.

5   ibid., p. 70.

6   JO Oviawe, 'How to rediscover the *ubuntu* paradigm in education', *International Review of Education*, vol. 62, 2016, pp. 1–10.

7   D Tutu, *No Future without Forgiveness*, Doubleday, New York, 2000.

# Index

If you want more resources on
how to practise gratitude or if you wish to
contact Kerry, please go to her website

**www.kerryhowells.com**

major st
PUBLISHING

We hope you enjoy reading this book. We'd love you to post a review on social media or your favourite bookseller site. Please include the hashtag #majorstreetpublishing.

Major Street Publishing specialises in business, leadership, personal finance and motivational non-fiction books. If you'd like to receive regular updates about new Major Street books, email info@majorstreet.com.au and ask to be added to our mailing list.

Visit majorstreet.com.au to find out more about our books (print, audio and ebooks) and authors, read reviews and find links to our Your Next Read podcast.

We'd love you to follow us on social media.

- linkedin.com/company/major-street-publishing
- facebook.com/MajorStreetPublishing
- instagram.com/majorstreetpublishing
- @MajorStreetPub

CPSIA information can be obtained
at www.ICGtesting.com
Printed in the USA
LVHW020817271021
701667LV00004BA/564